Seduction and Death in Muriel Spark's Fiction

Recent Titles in
Contributions to the Study of World Literature

Seduction and Death in Muriel Spark's Fiction

Fotini E. Apostolou

Contributions to the Study of World Literature, Number 107

GREENWOOD PRESS
Westport, Connecticut • London

Library of Congress Cataloging-in-Publication Data

Apostolou, Photeine.
    Seduction and death in Muriel Spark's fiction / by Fotini E. Apostolou.
        p.   cm.—(Contributions to the study of world literature, ISSN 0738–9345 ; no. 107)
    Includes bibliographical references (p.) and index.
    ISBN 0–313–31651–1 (alk. paper)
    1. Spark, Muriel—Criticism and interpretation.   2. Seduction in literature.   3. Death in
literature.   I. Title.   II. Series.
    PR6037.P29Z55   2001
    823′.914—dc21   00–069147

British Library Cataloguing in Publication Data is available.

Library of Congress Catalog Card Number: 00–069147
ISBN: 0–313–31651–1
ISSN: 0738–9345

First published in 2001

Greenwood Press, 88 Post Road West, Westport, CT 06881
An imprint of Greenwood Publishing Group, Inc.
www.greenwood.com

Printed in the United States of America

To Kostas

Everything is seduction and nothing but seduction.
—Jean Baudrillard
Seduction

If I had my life over again I should form the habit of nightly composing myself to thoughts of death. I would practise, as it were, the remembrance of death. There is no other practice which so intensifies life. Death, when it approaches, ought not to take one by surprise. It should be part of the full expectancy of life. Without the ever-present sense of death life is insipid. You might as well live on white eggs.

—Muriel Spark
Memento Mori

Contents

Acknowledgments

My particular thanks are due to all the people who, through their enthusiasm and support, helped me to complete this work. Words can't describe Jina Politi, without whose ideas my argument would have been completely different; an inexhaustible source of inspiration, Jina opened new horizons before me. Ruth Parkin-Gounelas made things much easier with her detailed and precise comments on my work; our discussions always bore fruit, as she had an amazing ability to urge me forward step by step. I would also like to thank Katy Douka-Kabitoglou, not only because her personal library was always available but also because she stood by me, ready to listen to my problems and offer her invaluable advice and experience. Karin Boklund-Lagopoulou, who never stopped believing in me, was a very supportive presence all these years. I am particularly grateful to Mr. Anargyros Heliotis, as he was the first to introduce me to Spark's fiction. The friendship of Katerina Kitsi-Mitakou was inestimable both during the first years, when she read my work, and during the last phase, because she was so supportive. Finally, our librarian, Fotini Stavrou, was immensely helpful.

Prologue

> [S]eduction is inevitable. No one living escapes it—not even the dead.
> For the dead are only dead when there are no longer any echoes from this
> world to seduce them, and no longer any rites challenging them to exist.
>
> —Jean Baudrillard
> *Seduction*

"Seduction is inevitable" as Jean Baudrillard states in his work *Seduction*. These three words alone capture, I believe, the essence of my argument, which will be an attempt to discover how seduction works in Muriel Spark's narratives, how it lures its objects into its domain and bewitches them.

Since the emphasis of this work is to be on seduction, I feel I should begin by clarifying what it was in Muriel Spark's writing that seduced me into writing about it.

When referring to Muriel Spark one always starts with her style, the best-known feature of her writing, since she is famous mostly for the extreme lightness of her tone, the delicate detachment that creates a chilling distance for the reader of her (mostly very short) fiction. It was this peculiar style of handling the most serious matters with such extreme, deadly serenity that first induced (or should I say seduced?) me into writing about her prose.

In contemporary fiction we witness a move toward a focus on the writing process itself, toward the mechanics of writing; the role of the author, the narrator, the character; the role of language as a structure that conditions and envelops human existence. Authors, suddenly uneasy about their "implied" role in narratives, try to redefine it by standing back and reflecting on their own and all previous texts—written or spoken—that have conditioned their writings.

Spark's work has often been studied in the light of metafictionality by modern critics like Patricia Waugh, Ruth Whittaker, Malcolm Bradbury, Gerardine Meany, and others. Her interest in the fictional process is revealed in her adoption of metafictional methods, whereby she exposes the structures that underlie the process of writing. What is of particular importance to these critics is Spark's preoccupation with metafictionality and plottings, which imprison her characters and mark their inability to escape writing.

Most of her critics have related Spark's interest in metafictionality to her religious beliefs, since it was her conversion to Catholicism in 1954 that signaled her entrance into fiction—until then she had written only poetry and some critical essays—through a process that I will discuss in more detail later. It was, therefore, to be expected that critics would focus their attention on her religion, which appeared to play such an important role in her fiction. As Patricia Waugh states in her influential book *Metafiction*: "The concern with freedom in both cases [Spark's and Fowles's] is . . . a consequence of the perceived analogy between the plot in fiction and the 'plot' of God's creation, ideology or fate. It is a concern with the idea of being trapped within someone else's order" (121). Waugh immediately goes on to relate this idea to the postmodern context of the imprisonment of language and signification: "At the furthest fictional extreme, this is to be trapped within language itself, within an arbitrary system of signification which appears to offer no means of escape" (121).

Evidently, Spark's Catholicism acts as a determining principle for critics who feel uncomfortable within a postmodern context. Most secondary works on Spark's narratives handle themes such as freedom, autonomy, and omniscience mainly in relation to her religion.

David Lodge, for example, who discusses Muriel Spark's omniscient narrators in his article "The Uses and Abuses of Omniscience: Method and Meaning in Muriel Spark's *The Prime of Miss Jean Brodie*," again touches on the issue of the relationship between Catholicism and omniscience: "The objections to orthodox Christian belief and to authorial omniscience in fiction are . . . essentially the same: that both involve a denial of human autonomy, of human freedom" (121). Freedom and autonomy, then, are inextricably bound to the doctrines of Catholicism and to omniscience.

Spark had a starkly complex religious and cultural background. The child of a Jewish father and a Protestant mother, she grew up in Scotland. Her marriage at an early age and her life in Africa, her divorce, and her work for the secret intelligence service of the British Foreign Office during World War II were significant cornerstones in her life. However, it was her conversion to Roman Catholicism that coincided, as I mentioned above, with a turning point in her life: her initiation into fiction and the finding of her voice as a writer.

Muriel Spark was intent on the idea of the right voice that would lead her to writing; she sought desperately to find a voice that would be hers, a voice which she managed to find only after her conversion at the age of 36. In the forty years following that event, she wrote ʼtwenty-one novels, many poems, plays, children's books, and short stories. She herself stated in 1961: "Nobody can deny I speak with *my own voice* as a writer now, whereas before my conversion I couldn't do it because I was never sure who I was, the ideas teemed, but I could never sort them out. I was talking and writing with other people's voices all the time. But not any longer. This is the effect of becoming a Christian" (Spark, "My Conversion" 61). Her works, however, have never been a clear proclamation of her faith, thus obstructing any efforts on the part of critics to associate her directly with her religion.

Gerardine Meaney, in her work *(Un)Like Subjects: Women, Theory, Fiction* (1993)—which focuses on the writings of Hélène Cixous, Luce Irigaray, Doris Lessing, Julia Kristeva, Muriel Spark and Angela Carter—has been the only one to study Spark's fiction from a feminist point of view. As she states in her introduction, "Muriel Spark . . . has never been associated with the feminist movement. Commentary on her novels had praised their capacity to push fiction to its self-reflexive limits and simultaneously to insist on fiction's right and ability to reflect on that which is outside fiction and even language" (10). Meaney focuses on Spark's novel *The Hothouse by the East River* in order to discuss woman's relationship to language and silence.

This work, too, shall attempt a new approach to Spark's texts, reading them from a wider postmodern/poststructural rather than a mainly feminist point of view. Postmodernism, with its emphasis on the intertextual games one can play with texts, can, as I hope to show, offer new readings of her work.

In Spark's writing there are infinite games that have not yet been discussed. Her novels and short stories foreground the play with texts, images, and spectacles in which her characters and her narratives are immersed and undone. Even her religion is embroiled in this playful atmosphere, becoming another structure that seduces and destroys with its regulations. In *The Takeover*, for example, Roman Catholicism is inserted, along with primitive cults, in a game with simulated orgies and rites where the most impressive spectacle will dominate the scene.

This book will focus on the "play" quality of Spark's writing and the seductive and destructive games associated with the process of construction: "seductive," because the power of existing structures is ever more present in her work, luring with its promise of dominance; and "destructive," since the introduction into these structures is associated with an alienation of the subject. It is one of the main concepts of poststructuralism that the subject is born into an already established symbolic system, which dictates its future position. In other words, it is this system that inscribes the individual.

For this view of Spark's work I am particularly indebted to Jean Baudrillard's theory of seduction. Baudrillard perceives seduction as a lure into an endless game with signification, which can redirect one's course, one's view of things. Therefore, I use this term to express the way certain structures entice the subject with their promise of power, because their manipulation would mean one is able to create constructs that imprison others within them. By the term "structure," I mean all those constructs that work through a system of rules and to which one has to conform; nevertheless, once manipulated they can grant one power over others (these can be: language, religion, education, the industry of the spectacle, etc.). However, in Spark's narratives her characters do not follow the rules obediently; rather, they experiment with existing structures, playing endless games with them that will lead to new paths, to different perceptions, and to new meanings.

How far is that possible, however? Can Spark's subjects escape the conditioning of structures and be free to play with them without being undone? Can one enter a set of given constructions without being alienated in them? This seems to be a utopia in Spark's texts, as the inevitability of alienation and death in this void that structures represent is foregrounded. The subject is not allowed to escape this alienation of the very structures that s/he uses to create other constructs.

We are led, therefore, into an endless spiral of seduction and death, where one enters a structure that envelops him/her in order to create a construct that will imprison others, who will, in their turn, desire to be enticed by this construct in order to enter and change it. All her characters seem to share a compulsion to repeat, as they continuously pursue the death brought by the structures. Spark's texts themselves follow the same pattern, seeking new games with given linguistic and literary structures.

I am interested, therefore, in this binary relationship with structures, which are both seductive and destructive. If we take the structure of the narrative, for example, we see Muriel Spark's work in the wealth of its intertextuality, as her subjects are placed in a continuous effort to construct their narratives in the multiplicity of texts that surround them. Everything acquires a flowing quality, where one text flows into another, one structure fades into another.

Within this realm of intertextuality the power of the text is foregrounded; the subject realizes its inability to exert any control over its constructs, which have a life of their own and haunt their creators to the final fall. The fact that many of the characters die before they are able to construct their narratives testifies to this "death of the author" in relation to the work, which stands distant from its creator, autonomous.

Moreover, as Spark's work progresses, it becomes more interested in modern constructs that further alienate the individual. It is not only the structure inside the narratives that is highlighted but also the outside, which follows the same pattern of seduction and alienation. Her texts focus on the world of the spectacle, which comes to dominate the scene of her narratives. Emphasis is now on another construct, the image, and its prevalence over its object—which is killed in representation—but also over its subject, since the allurement of his/her construction is so great that it comes to replace reality. Gradually, the real fades into its image, and simulation takes over, as representation seems increasingly to create rather than reflect "reality".

Seduction and Death
in Muriel Spark's Poetics

GAMES WITH STRUCTURES

Spark's entrance into fiction, as she describes it in her autobiographical work *Curriculum Vitae* (1992), is of particular significance. She went through a severe ordeal at the time of and immediately after her conversion. Because of under-nourishment and the use of Dexedrine "as an appetite suppressant" (*CV* 204), she had hallucinations—word puzzles, which fascinated her. She recalls, "As I worked on the Eliot book [at the time she was writing a book on the work of T. S. Eliot] one night the letters of the words I was reading became confused. They formed anagrams and crosswords. . . . It was difficult to convey how absolutely fascinating that involuntary word-game was" (*CV* 204). Seduced by these word visions, she set out to write about a similar experience in her first novel *The Comforters*, published in 1957, where the main female character, Caroline, who is trying to establish her identity as a writer, goes through a crisis of identity when she hears voices and the sound of a typewriter that seem to write her as a character in a novel: "'But the typewriter and the voices—it is as if a writer on another plane of existence was writing a story about us.' As soon as she had said these words, Caroline knew that she had hit on the truth" (*C* 63).

This fascination with voices, or, more generally, forms of discourse, appears in multiple forms throughout Spark's writing, starting from the voices of the narrator in *The Comforters*, going through the different voices of the caller of death in *Memento Mori* (1959); the voices of spirits in *The Bachelors* (1960), the voice of Joanna in *The Girls of Slender Means* (1963) reciting the Litany of the Day while trapped in a fire and finally burned; the voice of Margaret Murchie's mad uncle in *Symposium* (1990), where he serves as the "guru" of the family, guiding them in all the decisions they take; and ending with the voice of the director Tom Richards—in Spark's recent novel *Reality and Dreams*—which traps not only his actors in their roles but the director himself in his scenario.

There seems to be a continuous play with words, texts, voices, spectacles, rituals. The origin of the actual narrative of the novel or the short story is lost in a multitude of other narratives, forming part of the contemporary tradition to rewrite myths, stories, and histories—thus remaining within and, at the same time, without existing structures. In Spark's novels the reader is caught in the web of an endless *mise en abyme* of multiple texts, which, by fabricating a new, distorting perception of these "structures," reflects the fictional process.

The characters, immersed in multiple narratives, enjoy the plurality of discourse; they are fascinated by games of takeovers, where one incorporates the other in their fictions, slipping in and out of them with extreme ease. Writing, as Robert Young puts it in his essay "Post-Structuralism: An Introduction," ceases to be "a representation of something else [and becomes] the limitlessness of its own 'play'" (18). The case of Dougal Douglas in *The Ballad of Peckham Rye* (1960) is one of the most characteristic examples of this game with discourses. Dougal assumes a different discourse and a different personality with the same ease that he plays with his name, which he changes from Dougal Douglas, to Douglas Dougal (*BPR* 68) and to Dougal-Douglas "'spelt with a hyphen'" (*BPR* 75). Dougal indeed represents the discourse of postmodernism within the conservative realism of the community of Peckham Rye, which offers no fun. Like a small demon, always slippery like an eel, lost under his uncountable masks, Dougal seduces everyone with the lure of absence,[1] the endless games one can play with texts, the fun of moving freely in the multiplicity of fictions. The moment in the novel when this character dances with the lid of a dustbin is, I believe, indicative of the postmodern game with signs, whose nature is so arbitrary that they can be used to signify whatever one wants them to.

Then he placed the lid upside down on the floor, sat cross-legged inside it, and was a man in a rocking boat rowing for his life. . . . The dancers circled slowly around him while he performed a Zulu dance with the lid for a shield. . . .

Next, Dougal sat on his haunches and banged a message out on a tom-tom. He sprang up and with the lid on his head was a Chinese coolie eating melancholy rice. He was an ardent cyclist, crouched over handlebars and pedalling uphill with the lid between his knees. He was an old woman with an umbrella; he stood on the upturned edges of the lid and speared fish from his rocking canoe; he was the man at the wheel of a racing car; he did many things with the lid until he finally propped the dust-bin lid up on his high shoulder, beating this cymbal rhythmically with his hand while with the other hand be limply conducted an invisible band, being, with long blank face, the band-leader. (*BPR* 59–60)

This matches the poststructuralist theory of the text which, as Roland Barthes puts it, "turns away from the text as veil and tries to perceive the fabric in its texture, in the interlacing of codes, formulae and signifiers, in the midst of which the subject places himself and is undone, like a spider that comes to dissolve itself into its own web" ("Theory of the Text" 39).

The text, then, is a web with which one can play but into which one can also be dissolved. Its seductive and destructive power permeates Spark's fiction. Discourse, despite its prohibitions and its exclusions, still remains an object of desire, since it is synonymous with power: whoever masters discourse has an unlimited power to turn everything into an object of narrative. In Spark's world, as the appropriation of the text symbolizes the ultimate power of mastery, everyone desires authorship. However, this desire for a perfect manipulation of the structures that surround discourse is always deferred, as I will explain in the second chapter. Margaret Murchie in *Symposium* is incorporated within a deadly narrative, where she is doomed to be surrounded by death, without being able to exert any kind of control over it. When she finally decides to possess this deadly text, to create her own fictions and overpower the master narrative, she suddenly realizes her inevitable exclusion from the writing of the text and her final marginalization.

Spark's marginal characters are caught in a deadly embrace with the seduction of structures because they crave power, the mastery of the word, in a struggle for survival—a deadly game, where surviving depends on how far one can enclose others in one's fictions. This is the game of master-slave dominance in Spark's novels, which, as Gerardine Meaney suggests "are dominated by a struggle for authority, a struggle between conflicting models of authority" (187). And the outside is always present, always ready to seduce master and slave, like another Sirens' song aimed at Odysseus and his sailors.[2] In *The Ballad of Peckham Rye* Dougal Douglas personifies the evil force that sings the song of the Sirens, seeking to seduce both the employers and the employees of "Meade & Grindley, manufacturers of nylon textiles" (*BPR* 15), where he is hired, quite significantly, as an "Arts man."[3] For a moment he succeeds and it is he, as a personification of evil and the Arts—in other words, the outside—who seduces the narrative, bringing to mind Baudrillard's words that "Seduction is damned (but that is not the least of its charms)" (*The Ecstasy of Communication* 62). Eventually, master and slave return to their normal lives, and this evil man of Arts (the outside) is finally driven outside narrative, where he can thrive, as long as he does not disturb the structure: "The bonds with which [Odysseus] has irremediably tied himself to practice, also keep the Sirens away from practice: their temptation is neutralized and becomes a mere object of contemplation—becomes art" (Horkheimer 34).

Muriel Spark, from the beginning of her career as a novelist, showed a preference for amoral characters, for criminals who managed to transfigure the commonplace, for those whose imagination reaches beyond the usual, those who disturb the waters of serenity: they are the ones who can move beyond the constraints of good and evil, beyond the categorizations imposed by society or religion.

In Spark's fiction, evil has its own seduction that cannot be overlooked or avoided, even by the narrator. Characters that are supposed to be destructive have a charm that cannot be resisted. Miss Brodie in *The Prime of Miss Jean Brodie* is an obstinate, "fascist" teacher, who thinks she is the God of Calvin, as the narrator informs us, and wants to rule her students' lives. She even leads one to death. However, she cannot be resisted, as I will explain in the third chapter. Even Sandy who betrays her cannot escape the seduction of Jean Brodie, who moves within a realm that is beyond conventional dichotomies. As David Lodge suggests in his article "The Uses and Abuses of Omniscience," "Was Miss Brodie a good teacher or a bad teacher? The question is no easier to answer than the question of whether she was a good woman or a bad woman. In both cases the good and the bad are inextricably entwined" (130).

These are characters with exceptional qualities, with an imagination that sets them apart from all others. They use all the powers that are available to them, thus enjoying the full admiration of narrator and reader. According to David Lodge: "Miss Lockhart, . . . could 'blow up the school with her jar of gunpowder and would never dream of doing so'. (Miss Brodie, by implication, *would* dream of doing so.)" (131). Admiration is due to those capable of and willing to "transfigure the commonplace," to cast new light on old shadows. That is why Spark's fiction is so seduced by dark, evil figures that dominate her narratives. As Zarathustra states: "I love him who wants to create beyond himself, and thus perishes!" (Nietzsche 90–91). There are multiple allusions not only to criminals who seem to enjoy all the blessing of the gods but also to "witches" and "demons," who fascinate with their power of seduction.

Dougal—although he is the undoubted "authority" for a period in the text—is finally transformed into Art, a perpetual absent presence, caught within the discourse of the small community of Peckham, enclosed within the narrative of the novel. The outside is transformed into Art, and art always remains this outside that absorbs the lives of the characters and the narrative itself in a process of seduction, resulting in the complete destruction of a suppressing "reality" and an escape into the world of spectacle.

There are multiple structures that not only forbid access to discourse and monopolize it, but which also marginalize those who digress from a strict discipline within the boundaries of these structures. Foucault in "The Order of Discourse" presents us with this "order of discourse," the "conceptual terrain in which knowledge is formed and produced" (48), as Robert Young explains. This realm is determined by rules, systems and procedures which one has to respect, because otherwise s/he will be excluded from the power of discourse. Therefore, in order to constitute meaning, first you have to be constituted by the regulations of the order of discourse, and thus reproduce the system which defined you.

Foucault distinguishes between three groups of procedures which grant one mastery of discourse. First, there are the exterior social restrictions, which are "three great systems of exclusion which forge discourse—the forbidden speech, the division of madness and the will to truth" (55). Within these three systems the prohibition of speech applies mainly to sexuality and politics; the division of madness concerns the speech of the madman, which is rarely listened to and then only because it is believed to carry some hidden truth; and the third works as a foundation for the other two, resting on the division between truth and falsity.

Second, there are "the internal procedures, which function rather as principles of classification, of ordering, of distribution" (56). These are the following: the commentary principle, the author principle, and the discipline. Commentary restricts the openness of discourse by imposing a specific meaning on it; the "author principle" limits this openness by imposing an identity on the text, and the discipline by positing certain requisites for discourse—"a domain of objects, a set of methods, a corpus of propositions considered to be true, a play of rules and definitions, of techniques and instruments" (59).

Finally, there is a set of procedures that inhibit the control of discourse to those who do not adhere to them—ritual (gestures, behavior, circumstances), societies of discourse (for example, the book, the publishing system), the system of education, etc.

Following these strict limitations, Spark's characters are continuously excluded from discourse. Annabel, the actress in *The Public Image* (1968)—a novel I shall focus on in detail in the fourth chapter—is forced to flee the moment she deviates from the images that have been imposed upon her, that have seduced and absorbed her in the narrative. Fleur's novel in *Loitering with Intent* (1981) is not accepted for publication; in other words, she is not allowed to possess her own voice, because she refuses to conform to the regulations of "societies of discourse." Lise, in *The Driver's Seat* (1970), is confined, even if indirectly, to "the division of madness." In *The Prime of Miss Jean Brodie* (1961) Jean Brodie is linked to the discourse of fascism and therefore is marginalized and eventually eliminated. Hubert in *The Takeover* (1976) is imprisoned within his small cult until he decides to enter the dominant order, and so on.

Although these structures of discourse seem to be destructive and suffocating, they are also highly seductive. Different narratives and different fictions merge to create a series of "takeovers," where dominance depends on the most powerful "author." One structure is seduced into another; one author is trapped into another's narrative; and nobody seems to manage absolute control, or an ultimate liberation from the all-imposing structures that pervade the narratives.

Muriel Spark's fiction thus unmasks the strategies of the existing conditioning structures of power, revealing at the same time the illusory nature of any attempt to disengage from them. In her work we are led into a series of takeovers where power changes hands following the mastery of discourse. Needle, in the short story "The Portobello Road" (1958), not only returns after her murder by one of her friends but also manages to write her life story, trap her murderer in it, and finally take her revenge. As we shall see in chapter five, in *The Takeover*, a novel that foregrounds the continuity of all religions, Hubert, who rewrites the tale of Diana of Nemi and situates himself as the goddess's high priest and king of Nemi, is finally spoken for by Pauline—his secretary and a representative of the Pauline doctrine—who, embracing the Pauline doctrine, manages to transfer him into the structures of Roman Catholicism. In Spark's most renowned novel *The Prime of Miss Jean Brodie*, Miss Brodie destroys her students' image by imposing her own ambitions on their lives. The portraits of Jean Brodie's select group, all painted in her image by the art teacher at the school—deeply in love with her—testify to the imposition of her image upon her students:

[T]he picture was like Miss Brodie, and this was the main thing about it and the main mystery. . . . It was difficult to see how Teddy Lloyd had imposed the dark and Roman face of Miss Brodie on that of pale Rose, but he had done so. . . .

Then she saw a drawing lying on top of a pile on the work-table. It was Miss Brodie . . . ; on looking closer it proved to be Monica Douglas with the high cheekbones and the long nose. . . .

Eunice had worn the harlequin dress for a school performance. Small and neat and sharp-featured as she was, in the portrait she looked like Miss Brodie. (*PMJB* 100–101)

Jean Brodie in her prime "think[ing] she is the God of Calvin" (*PMJB* 120), tries to create her twelve students in her image, but is finally betrayed by one of them, only to be "resurrected" in the final lines of the novel by Sandy, the student who betrayed her: "'What were the main influences of your school days, Sister Helena? Were they literary or political or personal? Was it Calvinism?' Sandy said: 'There was a Miss Jean Brodie in her prime'" (*PMJB* 128).

Spark's work moves within a highly seductive relationship, a relationship between chaos and order, structure and destruction. Structure gives life and at the same time kills; it makes present and throws into absence. Her fiction at one moment plunges into order—the order of language, of narrative, plot—and at another into the void. Her characters are torn between a desire for freedom and the inevitability of imprisonment, seduced by disorder and de(con)struction but unable to withdraw altogether from structure, which is always there, always present with its absence and always ready to swallow them back into its deadly (dis)contents.

Most of her critics stress the fact that her narrators make revelations at the beginning of the texts, therefore emphasizing the inability of the characters to escape the plot, to escape the destiny that has already been written for them. This is the prison house of language, of writing that has the power to trap its subjects into its net of signification. In the majority of Spark's works, it is the same game that is played against the character and the reader—a game, however, that undoubtedly reflects the process of writing the text and being written by the text, enveloped by the work. It is this game of fiction, a game of death and life, absence and presence, that is highlighted in these works, as most of her fiction reflects this process.

At some point, just before the end of her fictions, it is as if the center is still there and really holds. But this is a false impression created only to be shattered a moment later. The king is still alive at the end in *The Takeover*, but what if he is? The Superman is long dead, since there is no room for creativity or originality. Hubert remains a king but is held captive in the sterile world of Pauline. In *Symposium*, the main female character is unable to impose her own scenario on a narrative that remains always outside her power, and in the short story "The Portobello Road," Needle has to die first in order to return and write her own life story afterwards.

With sudden revelations or no revelations, with unexpected twists in the narrative, the reader is always kept on the alert, sensing the danger but unable to know where the next blow will come from. The narrator builds up a relationship of mutual trust, only to reveal the rules of the game afterwards. One should have known better than to trust images, or to expect to find the "real" where there are only fictions. It is this fictionality that is foregrounded in Spark's narratives, as in the texts of many contemporary novelists, and one is left with the feeling that perhaps there is nothing but seduction that remains, that what matters in this journey to the unknown is the journey itself.

SIMULACRA AND THE FEMININE

As I will show in the second chapter, Muriel Spark in many of her works is interested in the idea of the attraction of the text, the pleasure one derives from the written work and from the experience of constructing fictions, "textasy," to use a word employed by Robert Young in an effort to convey the interaction between *jouissance* and signifiance: "'Jouissance' means enjoyment in the sense of enjoyment of a right, of a pleasure, and, most of all, of sexual climax. 'Jouissance' and 'signifiance' invoke the sense of an ecstatic loss of the subject in a sexual or textual coming—a textasy" (32).

It is the word as sign, emptied of its meaning, which becomes so seductive and empowering that everyone seeks to possess it. According to post-structuralism, it is not the subject who speaks language, but language that speaks the subject; it is the signifier—"the external, material letter of language" (Gallop, *The Daughter's Seduction* 19)—that dominates the speaking subject. Seduction, in the postmodern context, is exactly this force of the sign to fascinate and disorient; seduction lies in the power of signs to destroy the human impulse toward stable meaning. According to Jean Baudrillard, seduction is "a strategy of displacement (*se-ducere*: to take aside, to divert from one's path)" (*Seduction*

22), which "never belongs to the order of nature, but that of artifice—never to the order of energy, but that of signs and rituals" (2).

Seduction, then, is not used in the sense of enticing someone to have sexual intercourse but as a game. It can take various forms, depending on the object/subject that exerts it and can lead to various results. It can take the form of a woman (the seductress), the form of death, a gesture, a smell, a word—and one cannot avoid falling victim to the void that seduction represents. Consider the short story "The Go-Away Bird," where a girl who seems to have no origin and no end, is aware of the "go-away bird" from a very early age and is unable to escape the call's seduction. She is drawn toward this calling, which follows her wherever she goes with its absent presence, while she mysteriously falls for its enchantment:

Daphne was only half conscious of the go-away bird, even while she heard it, during the first twelve years of her life. In fact she learnt about it at school during natural history, and immediately recognized the fact that she had been hearing this bird calling all her life. She began to go out specially to hear it, and staring into the dry river-bed, or brushing round the orange trees, she would strain for its call; and sometimes at sundowner time, drinking her lemonade between Chakata and his wife on the stoep, she would say, "Listen to the go-away bird."

"No," said Chakata one evening, "It's too late. They aren't about as late as this." (GB 74)

The voice, therefore, cannot be traced directly to the bird, which most of the time cannot be heard by others. Daphne is the only one who has irredeemably connected her destiny to the calling of the bird and is to be chased by the calling to her death. During her short life she is always urged on by this call which, at some point, she fully incorporates, and she starts a gradual progress towards her chimeras, which prove unknown and hostile,[4] until she reaches her death: "She sat to rest on a stone, disturbing a baby lizard. 'Go'way. Go'way,' she heard. Daphne called aloud, 'God help me. Life is unbearable'" (GB 118). And in her death, which indeed comes when she calls for it, she loses her human nature, becoming a "buck" for her murderer: "Old Tuys was staggering home, exhausted, dragging something behind him. 'Go and pick her up,' ordered Chakata. 'I got me a buck,' said Old Tuys, looking with pride at the company. 'Man, there's life in the old dog yet. I got us a buck. . . . We have buck for dinner, man Chakata,' he said" (GB 119).

Daphne, then, falls prey to the seduction of the bird's calling. But, what does the calling stand for, if not the established structure that has imprisoned her and from which she cannot escape. Daphne was born into a duel between the two men—her uncle and Tuys—where she serves as the expiatory victim; the spectacle of her sacrifice is the one that will maintain the structure of the saga.

The seduction of signs gains new importance in Spark's later novels, where the spectacle dominates; the world of appearances turns meaning "upside down," as "meaning is vulnerable . . . to enchantment" (*Seduction* 8). Moving within this hyperreal universe, Spark's characters have perfectly adjusted their behavior to fit the new circumstances. And her fiction has also gradually changed, favoring survivors rather than martyrs, people who are lured by the glitter of gold, the artificial sign par excellence in the societies of the spectacle. Muriel Spark, having established a firm "center" for herself through her conversion, feels free to be seduced by the force of voices and appearances, by images and spectacles that abound in her texts.

Her "strategy of appearances" (*Seduction* 8) lures structure into destruction, death into life and vice versa. She thus manages to transform the "'everyday' language [that] endorses and sustains power structures through a continuous process of denaturalization whereby forms of oppression are constructed in apparently 'innocent' representations" (Waugh, *Feminine Fictions* 11) into a seductive discourse that displays and betrays these power structures through a continuous process of artificialization, whereby forms of oppression are deconstructed in evidently "guilty" images.

Muriel Spark introduces the reader into a new state, "the state of simulation, . . . in which we are obliged to replay all scenarios precisely because they have all taken place already, whether actually or potentially" (Baudrillard, *Transparency of Evil* 4). In all Spark's narratives, the reader, the characters, and the texts themselves seem trapped within a void, an endless imitation, what Jean Baudrillard calls "[an] interminable reproduction of ideals, fantasies, images and dreams which are now behind us, yet which we must continue to reproduce in a sort of inescapable indifference" (*Transparency of Evil* 4) until they are all finally devoid of meaning in this turmoil of reproductions and simulations.

It is significant that it is mostly women in Spark's work who let themselves be seduced by the signifier—words, texts, images, symbols—so that they manage to seduce others into their spectacles. Women, from their origins associated with the seductive games of spectacles, play the leading role in this game of seduction in Muriel Spark's narrative. After Lise, the central protagonist in *The Driver's Seat* and the most powerful seductress in Spark's fiction, gives to the voracious eyes of the public the spectacle of her voluntary murder, the police, the image of power par excellence, set out to explain it, to find goals and motives, victors and victims; they strive fruitlessly to give meaning to an absence, to what should remain merely an appearance. Lise evades any efforts to put her body/text within the limits of a "meaningful" discourse that has always marginalized her and that she now intends to seduce with her spectacle.

The relationship of women with appearances is worth exploring. Hasn't it always been a favorite practice among men to associate woman with the mask? Nietzsche wrote, notoriously, in *Beyond Good and Evil*: "[Woman] does not *want* truth: what is truth to a woman! From the very first nothing has been more alien, repugnant, inimical to woman than truth—her great art is the lie, her supreme concern is appearance and beauty. Let us confess it, we men: it is precisely *this* art and *this* instinct in woman which we love and honor" (164). Spark, I would argue, takes it upon herself to parody this idea. Woman, as I will show in the third and fourth chapters, is the true seductress, the one who can lure with her fictions and her masks. Artificiality is her "nature," and that is the role she is called to play. Spark takes this idea and carries it to its extreme, making her women and her marginal characters—homosexuals, "diabolic" individuals—dominate the power of appearances: Spark's women can play freely with simulations in the societies of the spectacle. Since they were given the weapon of masquerade they are allowed to manipulate it—in order perhaps to acquire "mastery of the strategy of appearances, against the force of being and reality" (*Seduction* 10).

Women psychoanalysts from very early have had much to say about seduction and appearances. Joan Riviere elaborated on Freud's seduction theory in her influential "Womanliness as a Masquerade" (1929). In this essay Riviere shows how the interplay of conflicts in modern woman is resolved through seduction. The focus is on the "manly" woman who is very successful in her job, but who has to resort to the power of appearances, to the masquerade, in order to prevent punishment from men for lacking in femininity. As she states: "Womanliness . . . could be assumed and worn as a mask, both to hide the possession of masculinity and to avert the reprisals expected if she was found to possess it" (33). Riviere's text highlights the void entailed in the masks woman is identified with: it is not only the "feminine" identity that is a mask; the "masculine" identity is also a veil, an artificial construct: "[Woman] has to treat the situation of displaying her masculinity to men as a 'game,' as something *not real*, as a 'joke'" (39, italics added).

In a parody of this close alliance between women and the masquerade, in Muriel Spark's work only those who can become objects of art, those who dominate appearances, are allowed to survive. The abbess in *The Abbess of Crewe* (1974), the tall dominant figure in her white robes, is a survivor because she has managed to master the new technology. Immersed in an intertextual game with fictions, this new Nixon figure, knows how to manipulate the image. Teaching her nuns all about computers, she has the monastery under her surveillance. Perfectly aware that the law depends on appearances, she works hard to construct her image, and she is the more praised by the narrator for her success in dominating the world of simulations.[5]

As Spark carries possibilities to extremes, man's "dangerous plaything," as Zarathustra describes woman in Nietzsche's *Thus Spoke Zarathustra*,[6] decides to dominate the scene with the weapons that were given to her. Women seduce and are seduced by the gaze of the camera, caught in the narcissistic discourse of their past, making continuous attempts to disengage themselves from the power of the images that have always depicted them in deforming ways. Annabel in *The Public Image*, a novel I will focus on in the fourth chapter, turns the game of appearances against those who first created it by dominating the images others had fabricated for her and with which they had framed her. It is in this novel that the spectacle of woman reaches its climax, until she completely embraces her artificiality.

Within this game of appearances, the gaze is magnetized by the distant object that the mass media offers, by the "sightless, shapeless depth, the absence one sees because it is blinding" (Blanchot, *The Space of Literature* 33). In Spark's narratives these lights dazzle and blind the gaze. According to Blanchot: "Fascination is solitude's gaze. It is the gaze of the incessant and interminable. In it blindness is vision still, vision which is no longer the possibility of seeing, but the impossibility of not seeing, the impossibility which becomes visible and perseveres—always and always—in a vision that never comes to an end: a dead gaze, a gaze become the ghost of an eternal vision" (*The Space of Literature* 32). Whenever the media enter the private world of the individual, they mark it with death, a total absence of being. The moment the camera focuses, the character dies, unable to escape the circle of death of the lens that closes in around him/her, and goes on and on, a series of murders over which the individual has no control. Spark's texts give the impression that there is always a hidden camera that the characters are aware of and that they are putting on an act for the sake of spectators, willing to kill themselves for the all-powerful image—"the Siren call of the black box" as Baudrillard calls it (*The Transparency of Evil* 57). Novels and short stories are replete with evil eyes "filled with voracity" (Lacan, "Of the Gaze as *Objet Petit a*" 115), eyes that can look, gaze, detect, reflect, kill. Absent cameras follow every move, photographing, recording, directing, framing.

The mass media are presented as voracious objects that eliminate the subject and the "real." In *The Public Image* the cameras transmit the picture of Annabel with her child and her neighbors mourning the death of her husband, a picture that is the sterile reenactment of similar scenes, where everything—feelings, people, objects—seems to be false, a representation that destroys any conception of the real or the true. Everything is revealed, offered to the masses for consumption, from the body of a woman who was raped and murdered in a park in *The Driver's Seat* to the private moments of a couple in their bedroom or in the kitchen in *The Public Image*. "It is no longer the obscenity of the hidden, the repressed, the obscure, but that of the visible, the all-too-visible, the more-visible-than-visible; it is the obscenity of that which no longer contains a secret and is entirely soluble in information and communication" (22) as Baudrillard puts it in *The Ecstasy of Communication*.

THANATOS

The characters, through their effort to master the image, to seduce it and possess it, are driven into the ecstasy of violence and death, trying to find in the end a new beginning: "[W]hoever kills himself is linked to hope, the hope of finishing it all, and hope reveals his desire to begin, to find the beginning again in the end, to inaugurate in that ending a meaning" (Blanchot, *The Space of Literature* 103). Spark's characters construct the spectacles of their deaths, which open the way to mastery of the ultimate moment. However, what does this moment signify if not another ending, a perpetual absence.

Whether one writes or is written, it is the same absence that dominates, the same seduction of death and the power that lies within that death. Many characters' deaths are written before they actually happen, since it seems that writing is the art of death—the art that should be practiced in cemeteries, as the character-author in *Loitering with Intent* very literally does, in a scene that will be discussed in more detail in the second chapter: "I sat on the stone slab of some Victorian grave writing my poem as long as the sun lasted" (*LI* 1).

Thanatos is undoubtedly one of the strongest drives in Spark's work, one always closely associated with the power of discourse and the desire for narrative. The relationship between language, desire and absence was initially focused on by Freud in *Beyond the Pleasure Principle*. The child in the *Fort/Da* game becomes the active agent only by repeatedly reproducing absence through discourse. On the one hand, the experience of the loss of the loved object is traumatic, but on the other hand, as the child "speaks" this lack, it manages to become the active agent, to control absence. Lacan's interpretation of this episode offers a new approach to the emergence of the subject into the Symbolic Order that opens the way to meaning but simultaneously leads to an alienation of the self. Through this process the child experiences a major loss, because of its alienation from the objects with which it previously identified.

Lise in *The Driver's Seat* is the literal illustration of this "textual desire," this deadly seduction of writing, as she willingly agrees to play the game of the narrator, thus partaking of the mastery of inscription.[7] Although she is perfectly compliant throughout the narrative—a narrative that seems to be hers as much as the author's—she cannot escape the ultimate seduction of the text: her sexual violation, that she has always detested and her final scream, when she dies, display the paradox entailed in writing. Writing is mastery and slavery at the same time. Her desire for a perfect unity with her body in death is deferred, giving birth to her text that will reiterate this deferral. The liberation it promises is a utopia; absence is always lurking behind the lines, a death brought by the structures to which one has to conform, in spite of always having resisted them.

Foucault discusses this dual relationship with discourse, which seduces with its promise of meaning—and thus power—and at the same time appalls with its threat of alienation in "The Order of Discourse": "[T]he prohibitions that surround it [discourse] very soon reveal its link with desire and with power. . . . discourse is not simply that which manifests (or hides) desire—it is also the object of desire; and since, as history constantly teaches us, discourse is not simply that which translates struggles or systems of domination, but is the thing for which and by which there is struggle, discourse is the power which is to be seized" (52–53).

This relationship of desire and abhorrence, distancing and immersion, beginning and end, presence and absence, death and life is what lies behind everything and what envelops everyone, including the narrator and the author, in the game of writing, the seduction of the word. The fictional work seems to possess a life of its own, ignoring any "authors," any narrators, or any other prior existence. In other words, it is as if the author herself is caught in this game of within and without, of absence and presence, speaking and being spoken for, writing and being written—seduced by the power of the word itself. Muriel Spark explains this process of seduction in an interview: "'... I like to go on and on and see how far they [her strong, diabolic characters] [will] go. The main thing is to be honest, to follow an idea through, wherever it's taking you'" (Frankel 451). This feeling is foregrounded in the novella *Not to Disturb* (1971), where three people are written into a scene of violent death by their servants who, as if by magic, knew exactly what was going to happen and wrote their masters' deaths in multiple forms (scripts, memoirs, interviews).

In other words, sometimes it is the narrative that takes over, that dominates the author, that "knows him not [and] closes in around his absence as the impersonal, anonymous affirmation that it is—and nothing more. . . . For isn't the writer dead as soon as the work exists?" (Blanchot, *The Space of Literature* 23). The days of domination are gone; there is no denying the author's death/absence from the work which "knows him not." It is not only the object of writing that is killed by the signifier, it is also the subject of the text, who realizes his/her absence from the work and the inevitable alienation brought by language.

This continuous game with the inside and the outside of the text, with absence and presence, is best revealed in "The Portobello Road" at the moment of Needle's murder:

He looked as if he would murder me and he did. He stuffed hay into my mouth until it could hold no more, kneeling on my body to keep it still, holding both my wrists tight in his huge left hand. *I saw* the red full lines of his mouth and the white slit of his teeth *last thing on earth*. Not another soul passed by as he pressed my body into the stack, as he made a deep nest for me, tearing up the hay to make a groove the length of my corpse, and finally pulling the warm dry stuff in a mound over this concealment, so natural-looking in a broken haystack. (PR 29–30, italics added)

In these seven lines, perfectly divided in the middle, we can see the literal alienation of the subject from the body: Needle can see the red full lines of George's mouth until the moment of her death, which initiates her external perception. The moment of her death draws the dividing line that splits the story in two: the silence before death and the narrative that follows it.

Death, then, marks both an end and a new beginning. Almost every case of violence exerted on a body initiates a new text, as if writing presupposes an elimination of the body. Frederick, Annabel's husband in *The Public Image*, who "jumped from [a church of the martyrs of St. John and St. Paul] to the foundations where they have placed the martyrdom of St. Paul" (*PI* 56), with this spectacular suicide, this overflow of images, drains death of its content, triggering other, more important significations. Until now, others have spoken for Frederick, but now, with his death, he speaks for himself for the first time. Nobody can die for him.

Death has given life to language, and it is death in Muriel Spark that continues not only to bear texts but also to imprison them. Her characters are chased by a strange longing for this death that is going to grant them access to discourse. Lise is suddenly freed from all constraints the moment she decides to kill herself in the most outrageous way. As Kirilov says "I will kill myself to affirm my insubordination, my new and terrifying liberty" (as quoted in Blanchot, *The Space of Literature* 97).

Death is perceived both as an exit from imprisoning rules and as an entrance into a new unknown structure. Therefore, in most cases death is a terrifying silence that promised a new beginning but failed to provide one. The desire for liberation and fulfillment is always deferred, always displaced to another fiction.

The body becomes in many cases the locus for the inscription of these fictions. And it is the desire for these texts that leads to the writing of deadly narratives on the body, narratives that mark the beginning of new texts, new plots that envelop one another in their deadly games. The desire for narrative, after all, according to Brooks, is a desire for the end, which maintains the movement of the reader through the pages of the texts. It is this end, surely, that is sought in Spark's texts and that marks a kind of Eros for Thanatos, a forward move that will create a beginning in the end after taking us through the detour of the narrative. As Peter Brooks comments in *Reading for the Plot*:

We emerge from reading *Beyond the Pleasure Principle* with a dynamic model that structures ends (deaths, quiescence, nonnarratability) against beginnings (Eros, stimulation into tension, the desire of narrative) in a manner that necessitates the middle as detour, as struggle toward the end under the compulsion of imposed delay, an arabesque in the dilatory space of the text. The model proposes that we live in order to die, hence that the intentionality of plot lies in its orientation toward the end even while the end must be achieved only through detour. (107–108)

The beginning is oriented from an end, a death that initiates narrative. The inscribed body is the beginning of the detour that, having come full circle, reaches again the end from which it began. In the novel *Territorial Rights* (1979), the narrative begins from and ends with the dead body of Victor Pancev who was killed by the Germans, vivisected by a butcher for two sisters who were his lovers and who buried the two parts of the body in their garden, each in her own part, so that they both possessed a part. The dead body, therefore, initiates the narrative that revolves around it, gives rise to plots and plotters, until it reaches its end at the same spot where it began, with Katerina and Eufemia, the two sisters, "cultivating their roses in the garden" (240), underlying the direct relation between discourse and death.

NOTES

1. Dougal is employed in the firm of Meadows, Meade & Grindley in order to combat "absenteeism": "Mr Druce said: '. . . You have to bridge the gap and hold out a helping hand. Our absenteeism,' he said, 'is a problem'" (*BPR* 17). However, instead of fighting absenteeism he repeatedly encourages the workers to take days off work, thus causing an increase of absenteeism in the factory.

2. The idea of the Sirens' song as related to the master-slave relationship is suggested by Horkheimer and Adorno in their work *Dialectic of Enlightenment*, pp. 32–38.

3. The reader is informed by Dougal himself that he had two horns on his head, which he had removed by plastic surgery.

4. She starts on a journey to England, to feel "at home" and to forget the African "go'way bird," but she feels even more alienated there; thus, she finally yields to the bird's call and returns to Africa, to the old structure of the duel between her uncle and Chakata, which will lead Daphne to her rendezvous with death.

5. Alexandra, the Abbess of Crewe, is one of these "evil" characters who fascinate with their wit, their unprecedented power to survive. As Ruth Whittaker observes: "Alexandra is determined to survive by turning herself into 'an object of art' (p. 125). . . . Appropriately, at the end of the novel she says in triumph, 'I am become an object of art, the end of which is to give pleasure' (p. 125). The novel does give pleasure, since a serious assessment of Alexandra's megalomania is not attempted, indeed is not admitted in any way by the narrator. And in the final paragraph, where a different perspective often appears or reasserts itself in Mrs. Spark's novels, she is given an elaborate and sustaining endorsement, which implicitly grants approval to her activities throughout the novel" (103–104).

6. Zarathustra, talking to an old woman about "old and young women," states: "The true man wants two things: danger and play. For that reason he wants woman, as the most dangerous plaything" (Nietzsche 91).

7. Gerardine Meaney in her work *(Un)like Subjects: Women, Theory, Fiction* makes the same point when she writes: "Lise's attempt to write her own script is defined by an acceptance that her fate is predetermined and that she is subject to a structure outside her control. Lise finds that her aspiration to 'authority' can be fulfilled only through complicity in the story of her own murder" (185).

2

Textasy: Writing and Being Written— Or, Seducing and Being Seduced

He would hope that, left to itself, the slight spark of life which he had communicated would fade; that this thing which had received such imperfect animation would subside into dead matter, and he might sleep in the belief that the silence of the grave would quench forever the transient existence of the hideous corpse which he had looked upon as the cradle of life. He sleeps; but he is awakened; he opens his eyes; behold, the horrid thing stands at his bedside, opening his curtains and looking on him with yellow, watery, but speculative eyes.

—Mary Shelley
Introduction to *Frankenstein*

This excerpt from Mary Shelley's introduction to *Frankenstein*, I believe, puts into a context the idea of the author's relation to his/her text, working on two levels at the same time. It is at this point that the "author's" chase by his creature begins, and it is at this moment that Shelley's pursuit by her text is phrased. Frankenstein's "text," a mixture of pieces from dead bodies, is brought to life and begins its wandering and the chase of its "author"—at times reading its own body, at other times demanding a change in the author's narrative, a participation in the "writing" of his destiny. Frankenstein, on the other hand, is both unavoidably drawn to his creation, his destiny inextricably bound to the monster's destiny, and repelled by its abnormality. Mary Shelley shares the same feelings for her text, feelings of astonishment at her creation and abhorrence at the monstrosity of her "hideous progeny" as she calls it.

The text in Muriel Spark's narratives has similar powers to enclose and trap, to change and manipulate. Her work plays with the idea of "the continuous subversion of the relation between writing and reading, between the sender and the receiver of the text" (Barthes, "Theory of the Text" 44). Spark's narratives are framed mirrors that reflect the struggle of the author, the character, and the reader to possess that which cannot be possessed, to seduce the narrative into their power, so that they may acquire the authority to imprison others in their texts. But how can the text be mastered? How can anyone command the absence that the text represents? The word has its own seduction, as the text envelops its subjects within its power while at the same time remaining always in the realm of the ungraspable—as Blanchot points out in *The Space of Literature*:

The writer seems to be the master of his pen; he can become capable of great mastery over words and over what he wants to make them express. But his mastery only succeeds in putting him, keeping him in contact with the fundamental passivity where the word, no longer anything but its appearance—the shadow of the word—never can be mastered or even grasped. It remains the ungraspable which is also the unreleasable: the indecisive moment of fascination. (25)

The struggle for possession of the text in Spark's work reaches its climax in the novel *Loitering with Intent*, where the author-character's manuscripts of her first novel go through a series of adventures before they can be published: one of them is destroyed by her future publisher; another is stolen by a reader, then usurped by the main character who has come to life and, laying a claim on the text, decides to change it while at the same time being immersed in it until, finally, the author manages to steal it back and publish it.

However, this process, instead of certifying the author's possession of her text, rather emphasizes the vicious circle entailed in writing, as the book is once again given to the reader to "steal," to seduce and be seduced by it. As Barthes explains in his essay "From Work to Text": "[N]o vital respect is due to the Text: it can be *broken* . . . : it can be read without the guarantee of its father, the restitution of the inner-text paradoxically abolishing any legacy. It is not that the Author may not 'come back' in the Text, in his text, but he then does so as a 'guest'" (161).

The author is only the medium through which this absence of language is mediated. Everyone is free to play with the text as they do in *Loitering with Intent*. All involved parties feel attracted by this game of possession, and the whole novel consists of plans for the appropriation of the text. The manuscript of Fleur's first novel is actually the source of all enjoyment in this novel, and all action is woven around it. Whole pages are devoted to the author's search of her room when she realizes that her manuscript has been stolen, her plans for repossession, and the search of her friend's apartment when she steals into it in order to locate her lost text.

The text, whether concrete—in the form of a manuscript—or abstract, is always absent in Muriel Spark's work, always in the realm of the ungraspable. In the case of *The Comforters*—her first novel—the text appears in the form of voices that can be heard only by the prospective author but cannot be traced, can never be transformed into a concrete presence. The main character, Caroline, hears these voices that are always accompanied by the sound of a typewriter writing what the voices are saying:

Caroline thought, "Well, he will ring in the morning." . . . On the whole she did not think there would be any difficulty with Helena.

Just then she heard the sound of a typewriter. It seemed to come through the wall on her left. It stopped, and was immediately followed by a voice remarking her own thoughts. It said: *On the whole she did not think there would be any difficulty with Helena.*

There seemed, then, to have been more than one voice: it was a recitative, a chanting in unison. It was something like a concurrent series of echoes. (*C* 42–43)

Caroline is after these voices that haunt her, trying to establish their presence that keeps evading her: "On the whole, she hoped the voices would return, would give her a chance to establish their existence, and to trace their source" (*C* 58).

Actually, it is this experience of sharing the voices of the absent author that marks Caroline's entrance into writing. As the narrative progresses, she gains insight; the voices gradually lead her into a deep knowledge that she can now communicate to others through her own writings. This long process of recognition and transcription of the voices is actually a process of self-recognition, the painful struggle of the author to get outside her narrative while being inside it, to write the text while she is being written by it: "Her sense of being written into the novel was painful. Of her constant influence on its course she remained unaware and now she was impatient for the story to come to an end, knowing that the narrative could never be coherent to her until she was at last outside it, and at the same time consummately inside it" (*C* 181).

This process of awareness and insight of the prospective author, this struggle of hers to find her own voice through the choir of voices of the "disembodied author" (*C* 162) who is within her and captures her in "the small crazy fragments of a novel" (*C* 160), goes through multiple stages before Caroline reaches the moment of enlightenment that will finally lead her outside the novel and inside her narrative.

The paradoxical relation between the author and the text acquires another dimension in the novella *Not to Disturb*, where the narrative has existed prior to the lives of its future authors, who, knowing its content, rewrite it in various forms and perform it, both in the novella, where they are the main characters, and in their own narratives, the movie scripts, where they will play the main parts. This text is the murder of the Baroness Klopstock and her secretary by the Baron Klopstock, and his suicide in the library of their castle in Switzerland in the middle of a storm.[1] Their servants—with Lister, the butler, having the leading role—know what is going to happen through some unknown and mysterious revelation that is never disclosed in the novella. They write their versions of this narrative/murder before it is actually performed. As we can see in the following quote from the text, this causes a continuous disturbance of the sense of time; Lister is talking about the murder in the past tense before it is actually performed: "Lister says impatiently. 'I am thinking.' Presently he turns on the recorder again, meanwhile glancing at his watch. 'The death of the Baron and Baroness has been a great shock to us all. It was the last thing we expected'" (*ND* 43).

The prospective *mise en abyme* of the servants' text foregrounds the inescapability of writing, or "the dominance of text over agents, plot over character" (121), to quote Ruth Whittaker. The seduction of writing cannot be avoided, as every character is drawn into the prewritten text and all sense of time is destroyed. "To write is" after all, as Blanchot comments, "to surrender to the fascination of time's absence . . . a time without negation, without decision, when here is nowhere as well, and each thing withdraws into its image while the 'I' that we are recognizes itself by sinking into the neutrality of a featureless third person" (*The Space of Literature* 30). Past, present and future are blurred, indistinct. This is further emphasized through the multiple allusions of the text to other narratives, like *The Duchess of Malfi*, *Frankenstein*, and *Jane Eyre*, and the result is an oscillation between what happened, what is happening, and what is going to happen.

"Of course he expected his dinner," Lister says. "But as things turned out he didn't live to eat it. He'll be arriving soon."

"There might be an unexpected turn of events," says Eleanor.

"There was sure to be something unexpected," says Lister. "But what's done is about to be done and the future has come to pass. My memoirs up to the funeral are as a matter of fact more or less complete. At all events, it's out of our hands." (*ND* 9)

The servants here are waiting for the secretary, who closes the triangle with the Baron and the Baroness, to come so that action can begin. However, there is absolute confusion with the tenses, as the characters refer to future events as though they have already taken place, with a constant interchange between future and past tense.

Since Lister's memoirs are complete, there is nothing that can be done; the text that seems to have preceded its author(s) is, after its writing, "out of [their] hands." In this absence of time everyone is drawn unavoidably into the written text, which has an autonomous and self-sufficient existence. The secretary's arrival and murder, in other words his adherence to Lister's text, is certain. The characters in *Not to Disturb* revolve around this narrative of no time, no origin and no end. Significantly, at the end of the novel, when the servants are trying to reach the late Baron Klopstock's brother in Brazil, there is a hint that the same narrative is about to begin at another place and in another time: "Clovis pushes his way through the mass of shoulders and reaches Lister. 'Phone call from Brazil,' he says. 'The butler won't fetch Count Klopstock on the phone. Absolutely refuses. He's locked in the study with some friends and he's on no account to be disturbed.' 'Leave word with the butler,' says Lister, 'that we have grave news and that we hope against hope to hear from the Count when morning dawns in Rio'" (*ND* 93). *Not to Disturb* foregrounds the labyrinth of narrative literature, which, according to Peter Brooks "is ever replaying time, subverting and perverting it"; "If the past is to be read as present, it is a curious present that we know to be past in relation to a future we know to be already in place, already in wait for us to reach it" (*Reading for the Plot*, 319).

The novella, with the center of action in the library, focuses on the seduction of the text, on the singularity of its power. Trying to overhear any conversations from the Library where the text-murder is to be played out, Lister observes: "'I hear no voices. . . . The books are silent'" (*ND* 44). In the end it is an abyss of intertextuality that remains, incomprehensible elliptical excerpts uttered in a void, simultaneously by the servants who are making their statements to the reporters:

Eleanor is saying, "Like a runaway horse, not going anywhere and without a rider."

Hadrian is saying, "The flight of the homosexuals . . ." to which his questioner, not having caught this comment through the noise, responds ". . . the flight of the bumble-bee?" "No," says Hadrian. . . .

"Togetherness . . ." says Irene.

Hadrian is saying, "Death is that sort of thing that you can't sleep off. . . ."

Pablo's voice cuts in, ". . . putting things in boxes. Squares, open cubes. It's a mentality. Framing them. . . ."

Eleanor says, "Like children playing at weddings and funerals. I have piped and ye have not danced, I have mourned and ye have not wept." (*ND* 91)

It is this seduction of words "uttered in a void," as Jean Baudrillard puts it (*Seduction* 75), that Caroline in *The Comforters* is trying to escape. In the beginning, the voices speak and write what went through Caroline's mind in the moment before they were heard, but then they move away from her and she can hear the thoughts of the author who is writing the narrative, giving her a glimpse of the future text that will write her life: "It had already started its chanting. She switched on the light and grabbed her notebook and pencil. She missed the first bit, but she got: '... *next day by car, though Lawrence's M.G. was due for repair, instead of going by train. This was owing to their getting up late and frittering the day in talk, first about poor Eleanor, as they agreed she was, then about themselves. Click. Click*'" (*C* 93).

Author, reader, and character simultaneously, Caroline needs to assert her free will, her resistance to the text that drowns her in its plot. Her attempts to evade this writing fail, confirming the inescapability of the seduction of the narrative. As soon as Caroline realizes the "truth," that "a writer on another plane of existence [is] writing a story about [them]" (*C* 63), she begins a struggle for mastery over the narrative: "'The narrative says we went by car; all right, we must go by train. You do see that, don't you, Lawrence? It's a matter of asserting free will.' He quite saw. He thought, 'Why the hell should we be enslaved by her secret fantasy?'" (*C* 97).

Caroline will not assert her autonomy, nor will she find her voice unless she disentangles herself from the text that is imprisoning her. This critical moment of liberation is depicted through her struggle with her evil creation, Mrs. Hogg—a woman who is constantly chasing Caroline with accusations about her morality—when the latter falls into a river and drags Caroline down into the depths of the muddy waters.

Caroline struck her in the face. "Hold on to my shoulders," she shouted. "I can swim." But the woman in her extremity was intent on Caroline's throat. Caroline saw the little boat bobbing away downstream. Then her sight became blocked by one of Mrs Hogg's great hands clawing across her eyes, the other hand tightening on her throat. Mrs Hogg's body, and even legs, encompassed Caroline so that her arms were restricted. She knew then that if she could not free herself from Mrs Hogg they would both go under.

. . . The woman clung to Caroline's throat until the last. It was not until Mrs Hogg opened her mouth finally to the inrush of water that her grip slackened and Caroline was free, her lungs aching for the breath of life. Mrs Hogg subsided away from her. God knows where she went.

Caroline had the sense of being hauled along a bumpy surface, of being landed with a thud like a gasping fish, before she passed out. (*C* 196–97)

Mrs. Hogg, who seems to be Caroline's creation, since she comes alive only through Caroline's involvement,[2] makes her absence ever more present in the narrative. Until her final disappearance in the muddy waters, the text is continuously playing with this characteristic of hers to be very present while always absent. There are quite a few references to Georgina Hogg's absence in the novel. Her ex-husband is the first one to speculate on this fact: "As he mounted the stairs towards [Georgina's room], he heard the swift scamper of mice, as if that part of the house was uninhabited" (*C* 140). Then, there comes another comment on the part of one of Caroline's friends and Mrs. Hogg's protectress, Helena, who states: "'I am beginning to think that Georgina is not all there'" (*C* 154). This is followed by the narrator's statement that "as soon as Mrs Hogg stepped into her room she disappeared, she simply disappeared. She had no private life whatsoever. God knows where she went in her privacy" (*C* 156). Then, there is Caroline's perception of this absence, when Mrs. Hogg goes to Caroline's house: "For a second Caroline got the impression that nobody was there, but then immediately she saw the woman standing heavily in the doorway and recognized the indecent smile of Mrs Hogg" (*C* 181), which is followed by a discussion between Helena and Caroline: "'[I]t's not what she says, it's what she is.' 'She's not all there,' said Helena. Presently Caroline sprayed the room with a preparation for eliminating germs and insects" (*C* 182). The climax comes before the final disappearance with her death when, during the drive to the riverside with Helena and the Baron, she disappears and reappears in the car, and then disappears again on the riverside ("'Spirited away,' said Lawrence remarkably" [*C* 193]), until she finally re-appears in the middle of the storm on the opposite bank of the river. Through this *mise en abyme* Muriel Spark manages to highlight the text's influence on its author; in the same way that Mrs. Hogg's absence is present in her author's life, so is Caroline's "unreckoned influence" commented on by the narrator of the novel.

In Muriel Spark's work we witness this retroactive relationship between author and text from her first novel, not only at the level of the inner text (Caroline and Mrs. Hogg) but also at the level of the outer text, in the relationship between the author-persona of the novel and her construct, Caroline, who keeps intervening in the writing of the text. The narrator in *The Comforters* often comments on Caroline's involvement in the writing process: "Caroline among the sleepers turned her mind to the art of the novel, wondering and cogitating, those long hours, and exerting an undue, unreckoned, influence on the narrative from which she is supposed to be absent for a time" (*C* 137).

Instead of the author haunting the character, as the novel progresses it is the character, Caroline, that begins to haunt the author. The voices that have imposed their presence on her are consumed, digested, and suddenly regurgitated, until it is Caroline's voice that begins to be recorded by the narrator: "'The *Typing Ghost* has not recorded any lively details about this hospital ward. The reason is that the author doesn't know how to describe a hospital ward. This interlude in my life is not part of the book in consequence.' It was by making exasperating remarks like this one that Caroline Rose continued to interfere with the book" (*C* 161, italics added).

The roles are reversed and now it is the character's turn to dematerialize the author, to reduce him/her into a "Typing Ghost," whose powers are rather limited and who can indeed be overpowered by his/her creatures. The words, then, have the power to intervene in the narrative, to change its course, much to the surprise and evident disapproval of the narrator who sees the characters interfering in the text. It seems that this author-persona shares Caroline's surprise when the latter realizes that she is being written as a character into a novel. The mystery of the relationship between the author and the text is further complicated by the question that arises at the end of the text: Who is the author of this narrative? The two texts—the one in italics that transcribes the voices and the actual text of the narrative—merge in the novel that Caroline is about to write, or has already written. *The Comforters* ends with a letter from Lawrence to Caroline, commenting on her notes for the first novel—the notes that she kept after she heard the voices—and expressing his discontent at "being a character in [her] novel" (*C* 203). Lawrence, who finally tears his letter "into small pieces, scattering them over the Heath where the wind bore them away" (*C* 203), does not "foresee his later wonder, with a curious rejoicing, how the letter had got into the book" (*C* 204). These are the final words of the novel that further complicate the question concerning the origin of the text and underline the vanity of trying to disentangle the complexity of the writing process.

There is hardly a Spark novel that does not focus on the power of writing, especially in the many narratives where the main character is a woman writer— perhaps a narcissistic image of Spark herself—with whom Spark, through multiple *mises en abyme*, shares the experience of writing, constructing narratives that in their turn construct the author. Her texts are highly self-reflexive in the sense that "conscious of their literariness, [they] 'narrativize' it and strive, by a permanent or occasional reference back to themselves, to reveal the law underlying every linguistic creation" (Dällenbach 48). The reader cannot distinguish between the "about" and the text, as "reality" is immersed into fiction. In *The Prime of Miss Jean Brodie*, Sandy writes stories and places herself in them, enacting them, thus following Jean Brodie's example. The "real" is always immersed in fictions, which are overpowering: fictions encompass "reality" and pursue their creators, like images that are imposed on the "real," which disappears behind the power of the image.

Jean Brodie lives her life through her fictions and reformulates her past according to the new fictions she creates.[3] Following her example, her students, "fascinated by this method of making patterns with facts" (*PMJB* 72), write their own stories, in which they envelop their teacher. In the same way that she distorts her past and her students' present with her fictions, they in their turn distort her romantic fictions with their adolescent text. The burial of Miss Brodie's romance by her students Sandy and Jenny after they write it, signals the next stage in their lives, in a natural process that they follow, suddenly realizing that Jean Brodie has never overcome the romantic stage in her life; that is why she has to be killed, and her fictions turned against her. Even fascism is romanticized in Jean Brodie's life, replete as it is for her with images of grandeur:

"These are the fascisti," said Miss Brodie, and spelt it out. "What are these men, Rose?"
    "The fascisti, Miss Brodie."
    They were dark as anything and all marching in the straightest of files, with their heads raised at the same angle, while Mussolini stood on a platform like a gym teacher or a Guides mistress and watched them. Mussolini had put an end to unemployment with his fascisti and there was no litter in the streets. It occurred to Sandy, there at the end of the Middle Meadow Walk, that the Brodie set was Miss Brodie's fascisti, not to the naked eye, marching along, but all knit together for her need and in another way, marching along. (*PMJB* 31)

Fascism is fictionalized in this continuous oscillation between the real and the imaginary, the within and the without, and in its fictionalized form it seduces the "reality" of the students and their teacher.

This oscillation seems to be played out on another level as well, that of the author and her narcissistic others, as I explained above—women who write narratives, struggling to find the "voice" that will give them mastery over self and language—that fill Spark's fiction. Her work is replete with women who write and are written by their fictions, starting from Caroline in *The Comforters* and moving through almost four decades of novels: Jean Brodie and Sandy Stranger in *The Prime of Miss Jean Brodie*, Sybil in "Bang-bang You're Dead," Needle in "The Portobello Road," Annabel in *The Public Image*, Lise in *The Driver's Seat*, Elsa in *The Hothouse by the East River*, the abbess in *The Abbess of Crewe*, Maggie in *The Takeover*, Fleur in *Loitering with Intent*, Effie in *The Only Problem*, Margaret in *Symposium*, Beate Pappenheim/Wolf/Anna O. in *Aiding and Abetting*, and finally, Muriel Spark the author-persona in her autobiographical work *Curriculum Vitae*. These narcissistic reflections become the focus of attention in the Sparkian text, thus creating highly self-reflexive narratives that blur the border between the within and the without of her texts.

Spark's novel *Loitering with Intent*, holding the mirror to itself—to the whole process of writing, reading, listening, criticizing, publishing—makes it very difficult to define any such dividing lines. Fleur, the author-narrator-character, writes and narrates an autobiographical narrative that is about the writing of a novel, which she reads to a listener who narrates it to others, and feels free to confiscate it, while other readers manipulate and distort it. Critics read and condemn it, publishers see and reject it, characters possess and rewrite it, or rewrite themselves in it, and finally, with the publication of Fleur's text, the story has come full circle and can start all over again, as the seduction of the sign is ever more present in the narrative.

Spark's characters are, in one way or another, inextricably bound to some text that seduces them into its realm but from which they are trying to escape or which they are trying to envelop through the power of other texts. These are present in her works in the form of narratives, pictures, and games that unavoidably draw the protagonists into their plottings. Needle in "The Portobello Road" is seduced by the power of the photograph that her friend George takes, thus giving her a name and a text that frame her. Sybil in "Bang-bang You're Dead" is seduced by a childhood game, where she is doomed to be shot; or, perhaps, as the narrative suggests later on with a reversal of the plot, she is seduced by the story that her name alludes to, that of the Cumaean Sibylla who, having refused the love of the god, is doomed to eternal life. This seduction follows Annabel in *The Public Image*, Hubert in the *Takeover*, Harvey in *The Only Problem*, Tom Richards in *Reality and Dreams* and many other characters in Spark's narratives, ending with "Lucky" Lucan and Beate Pappenheim in Spark's most recent novel *Aiding and Abetting*, whose lives are overtaken by their "true" stories, continuously oscillating between the "real" and the "fictional."

In *Loitering with Intent* this seduction of the sign gains another dimension as the text comes to life. Fleur Talbot, the writer, remarks at one point: "I had my unfinished novel personified almost as a secret companion and accomplice following me like a shadow wherever I went, whatever I did" (*LI* 60). But her finished novel also comes to life. The words on the page suddenly acquire a life of their own, as Fleur realizes: "Sometimes I don't actually meet a character I have created in a novel until some time after the novel has been written and published. And as for my character Warrender Chase himself, I already had him outlined and fixed, long before I saw Sir Quentin" (*LI* 25). Sir Quentin, on the other hand, is determined to enact the character—"I saw before my eyes how Sir Quentin was revealing himself chapter by chapter to be a type and consummation of Warrender Chase, my character" (*LI* 60)—and haunt his creator, Fleur, who at one moment exclaims: "It seemed quite unlikely that my own novel could be entering into my life to such an extent" (*LI* 180). Possibly haunted by the image of Mary Shelley's *Frankenstein,* Spark is often preoccupied with the idea of the text coming to life and pursuing the author, who is desperately trying to get hold of it and reassert her power.

The author has breathed life into evil that will haunt her to the end. Like Frankenstein who, "ha[ving] been the author of unalterable evils" (Shelley 355), experiences the threat of imminent death from his own creation, Fleur Talbot also senses danger from her own creature, Sir Quentin Oliver—the reincarnation of her character Warrender Chase. He threatens to destroy her novel, which would inevitably signal her own destruction, as it is through her text (her art) and for her text that she lives.[4] The text that Fleur Talbot, the main character, writes is manipulated through the narrative: changing hands, it passes from the author to the reader, to the publisher, to her main character—who decides to rewrite it—and finally back to the author.

What is the destiny of Fleur, the author, however? The truth is that she is never free. She is always to be haunted, enveloped in her own creation, chased by her own words, her own creatures, her own Warrender Chase, which is both the title of the novel and the name of its main character. It is worth referring to the significance of this name, which suggests both the "chase" that will follow— with its many allusions to *Frankenstein*—and the wandering (Warrender) quality of the character and its author, who are lost in the web of their interrelationships.

The words on the page suddenly escape the author's control. Like the "fiend" of Frankenstein, once created, they move beyond the reach of their creator and assert their private existence, their autonomy. Fleur's characters make extreme efforts to escape her conditioning, but an inevitable force always leads them back to their creator—the mother who has given them life but at the same time deprived them of it. The evil Fleur has created in the face of her character, Warrender Chase, becomes real and chases her to the final fall, aiming to destroy her by gaining possession over the narrative, which he believes to be his, since he is the main character. The relationships become further complicated as Sir Quentin Oliver—or Warrender Chase—on the one hand tries to escape the narrative, to change it and rewrite it,[5] while on the other hand he is so anxious to enact it, to be immersed in it, that he can never escape. As Fleur observes: "I think he's putting my *Warrender Chase* into practice. He's trying to live out my story" (*LI* 177).

While the author herself is repelled by this evil creation of hers, it is evident that not only did she give birth to him, she is also inescapably drawn to her creature[6] in the same way that he is simultaneously attracted and repelled by her text. The result is that they pursue each other's narratives to the end, to the final destruction that is going to bring liberation to the destroyer, following again in the footsteps of Mary Shelley's *Frankenstein*, on which Spark comments in her work on Mary Shelley: "There are two central figures—or rather two in one, for Frankenstein and his significantly unnamed Monster are bound together by the nature of their relationship. Frankenstein's plight resides in the Monster, and the Monster's in Frankenstein. . . . Frankenstein is perpetuated in the Monster" (*Mary Shelley* 161).

Pursuit is a common theme in many of Spark's works, since possession of the text means victory, liberation, mastery. All this, as we saw, leads to continuous games with texts and to an endless *mises en abyme* of narratives. Muriel Spark slides in and out of genres, using autobiographies, novels, newspaper articles, films, surveys, religious texts, and poetry. The author, evidently, is free to "loiter with intent," to unearth hidden narratives, deadly secrets, evils that may be of interest to her. In *Loitering with Intent* and other novels, all these mirrorings result in a constant interchange of identities, where one text reflects the other, one story is inserted into the other, one author is written by another. These reflections which, according to Dällenbach, "cannot be captured in a single mirror, but [are] projected through various filters, in a series of mirrors that open up dizzying perspectives" (34), lead to a series of questions that constantly perplex the reader of Muriel Spark's work, lost as s/he is in the multiple *mises en abyme*. Whose is the text, then? Whose is the voice that speaks and whose is the hand that writes?

As in so much fiction since Henry James, the constant undermining of the role of the omniscient narrator further complicates the issue. As Patricia Waugh observes: "Muriel Spark uses the omniscient-author convention, not benevolently to signpost the reader's way through the text, but to express a disturbing authority whose patterns are not quite so easy to understand" (*Metafiction*, 74). The author-persona in *The Comforters* often admits her defeat by her own creature, Caroline, who exerts an "unreckoned influence" on the novel. In *The Prime of Miss Jean Brodie*, Sandy's eyes are the eyes of the reader, since it is Sandy who is established as a "perceiving consciousness in the novel" (Lodge 128). Lodge also points out that "Sandy is not . . . a totally reliable point of reference. . . . Her eyes, as well as symbolising her shrewdness and perceptiveness, also symbolize less attractive qualities. They are described as 'pig-like eyes' (13) and as 'tiny eyes which it was astonishing anyone could trust' (100)" (128). Her perception then is devaluated and the reader is discouraged from trusting the novel's point of view. The narratives are subject to distorted visions, to the faults of different angles of perception.

In *Loitering with Intent* everyone involved in the novel perceives Fleur's narrative from different perspectives. Each lays claim to it until the climactic moment of repossession by the author when she finally finds the stolen manuscript of her novel: "[M]y fingers had found a package, the size of a

London telephone directory, wedged at the bottom of the ghastly black bag. Out I whisked that package in a flash, and in another flash had opened it. My *Warrender Chase*, my novel, my Warrender, Warrender Chase; my foolscap pages with the first chapters I had once torn up and then stuck together; my *Warrender Chase, mine*. I hugged it. I kissed it" (*LI* 169). Doesn't this emphasis on the possessive pronouns seem rather exaggerated? And doesn't it rather reveal a vain struggle for possession on the part of the author, instead of underlining actual possession? Spark here seems to be playing with the idea of mastering a "sign" that signifies "absence" rather than "presence," loss rather than possession.

What is more, the text seems to have been there prior to Fleur's existence. It was there in the form of a dead body she resurrected. She is the mother-creator, another Mary Godwin/Shelley sitting by her mother's (Mary Wollstonecraft's) grave and reading,[7] digging graves so as to bring her "hideous progeny" to life, constructing it from pieces here and there and piecing it together—like Frankenstein who is bound to haunt graveyards in order to become the "author of evils," with his patchwork of dead matter, coming from the violation of dead bodies.

It is this relationship of the writer with death, this continuous struggle with death, and this affiliation between writing and dying that is depicted in the beginning and end of the narrative, when Fleur is found in a Victorian graveyard on that symbolic date, writing poems. And, it is between these moments that she speaks her story, where her characters and readers come alive and chase her:

It was right in the middle of the twentieth century, the last day of June 1950, warm and sunny, a Friday, that I mark as a changing-point in my life. That goes back to the day I took my sandwiches to the old disused Kensington graveyard to write a poem with my lunch, when the young policeman sauntered over to see what I was up to. . . . I asked him: suppose I had been committing a crime sitting there on the gravestone, what crime would it be? "Well, it could be desecrating and violating," he said, "it could be obstructing and hindering without due regard, it could be loitering with intent." (*LI* 200)[8]

The narrative begins and ends in a Victorian cemetery, where the reader is, for the first time, acquainted with Fleur as an author. Her existence begins in the graves and ends with the graves. The character-author of *Loitering with Intent* is chased into graveyards by her words: "I took my sandwiches to the old disused Kensington graveyard to write a poem with my lunch." It is as though the presence of the graves gives her the life that she needs in order to exist as an author and as a character in the narrative, since it is her day in the graveyard that signals the beginning of her text.

Unable to avoid this seduction of the dead, Fleur discovers life in death, following Frankenstein's example: "I succeeded in discovering the cause of generation and life; nay, I became myself capable of bestowing animation upon lifeless matter" (312), capable of "renew[ing] life where death had apparently devoted the body to corruption" (314). For her, art is found there, in dead matter, which she has to animate. In her hands the autobiographies of the members of the Autobiographical Association—which she considers "inventions of her own" (*LI* 36)—take new life, like the autobiography of "Sir Eric Findlay, K.B.E., a sugar-refining merchant whose memoirs, like the others, had not yet got farther than Chapter One: Nursery Days. The main character was Nanny. I had livened it up by putting Nanny and the butler on the nursery rocking-horse together during the parents' absence, while little Eric was locked in the pantry to clean the silver" (*LI* 36–37).[9]

This lure of the dead is also noted by another critic of Spark's work, Malcolm Bradbury, who points out in his essay of 1973 "Muriel Spark's Fingernails": the phase of the author's work that includes *The Public Image*, *The Driver's Seat* and *Not to Disturb* consists of "novels of ending" (249), where "people arise at the last, *from* the last" (250). This awareness reaches its climax in "The Portobello Road," where we witness the "realization" of the "metaphoric," the "impossible possibility," or "the possible impossibility." In this narrative the game Spark plays between seduction, death, and writing is highlighted. Narrated in the first person by a dead author, it leaves the reader suspended in midair, as Needle addresses the reader from the realm of the uncanny, the absent. Spark turns the death of the author, of which Barthes and Blanchot spoke metaphorically,[10] into a literal nightmare; the paradox of writing is realized in the form of Needle, a literal absence that plays the role of the metaphorical absence of the author and the narrator. The reader finds him/herself in a ghost story that does not wait to be narrated by a third person but is written by the ghost herself. As Needle herself clarifies towards the beginning of the story, much to the astonishment of the reader, "I must explain that I departed this life nearly five years ago. But I did not altogether depart this world."

Indeed, Spark's characters in these novels and many others arise from the dead and haunt her texts, as she cannot escape the writing of the dead. However, who can deny the death impulse immanent in all novelistic characters? Or who can deny the death drive that leads all authors to writing? Undoubtedly, the author is dead as soon as the work of art comes into being, but Spark is also interested in what takes place before that death, before the end of the work of art, during the process of writing, or even before it begins.

The author-characters' relationship with their works is a relationship of love and hate, death and life, presence and absence; their "monstrous creatures" are all too dear to them, all too attractive to be expelled. Fleur, being a woman and a writer in the twentieth century, can go on her way rejoicing, can celebrate her "hideous progenies" without having to apologize for them, or reject them. The women artists in Spark's works, all these female author-personae that she employs in her fiction, have to dive deep into death to find life, and most of them have to go through a death of the body in order for their texts to materialize. Death for them is a calling, a terrifying *memento mori* that creates no fears, no regrets; rather, it signifies the unavoidable seduction of the text, which lures its victims into its embrace and undoes them.

NOTES

1. There is a clear allusion here to the murder of Frankenstein's wife in Mary Shelley's *Frankenstein*, with the storm raging outside the Austrian inn, situated next to Lake Como near the Alps. In both cases, it is a "text" that intervenes between the couple. In the case of *Frankenstein*, the "monster"—Frankenstein's "text"—kills Frankenstein's wife and with her death he marks his creators death too. Frankenstein's life is terminated with this murder, after which he is transformed into a "monster" himself, seeking revenge. In Spark's novella, it is the "secretary," the transcriber of the Baron's "texts," that intervenes and leads to the couple's destruction.

2. As the narrator suggests, Mrs. Hogg was first perceived, or perhaps conceived, by Caroline: "Wasn't it she [Caroline] in the first place who had noticed with revulsion the transparent blouse of Mrs Hogg, that time at St Philumena's? It was Caroline herself who introduced into the story the question of Mrs Hogg's bosom" (*C* 139).

3. As the narrator informs us in *The Prime of Miss Jean Brodie*, Jean Brodie reformulates the story of her past love affair in order to fit her present attraction to the music teacher and mostly to the one-armed art teacher at school: "Miss Brodie's old love story was newly embroidered, under the elm, with curious threads: it appeared that while on leave from the war, her late fiancé had frequently taken her out sailing in a fishing boat and that they had spent some of their merriest times among the rocks and pebbles of a small seaport. 'Sometimes Hugh would sing, he had a rich tenor voice. At other times he fell silent and would set up his easel and paint. He was very talented at both arts, but I think the painter was the real Hugh'" (*PMJB* 71–72).

4. There is an allusion here to Benvenuto Cellini's autobiography—often quoted in *Loitering with Intent*—which emphasizes the importance of art for the artist. The feeling of rejoicing frequently experienced by Fleur is taken from Cellini's autobiography, as is the idea of the importance of writing about one's art that is highlighted at the beginning of his *Autobiography*: "No matter what sort he is, everyone who has to his credit what are or really seem great achievements, if he cares for truth and goodness, ought to write the story of his own life in his own hand"(15).

5. After reading some pages of Sir Quentin's diary, Fleur states the following: "[W]hat infuriated me more than anything in these scraps of Quentin Oliver's diary was this last entry, 2nd May. It was straight out of *Warrender Chase*, where I make my character Proudie find the absurd letter to the Greek girl who thought it far from absurd" (*LI* 188).

6. Although she takes the decision to stay away from Sir Quentin Oliver, she finds that she is again and again drawn back to him: "I had twice decided not to return to Hallam Street, and now for the second time I was obliged to go back" (*LI* 163).

7. As Muriel Spark informs us in her work on Mary Shelley, "Mary formed the habit of taking her books to her mother's grave in St Pancras Churchyard, there to find some peace after her irksome household duties, and to pursue her studies in an atmosphere of communion with a mind greater than the second Mrs Godwin's. And it was there, before long, that she was meeting Shelley in secret" (*Mary Shelley* 19). Therefore, the cemetery for Mary Shelley was a place for contemplation, study, love, and creation through Mary's contact with her mother's spirit.

8. Frankenstein's loitering in Mary Shelley's novel is indeed "with intent": "I pursued nature to its hiding places. Who shall convince the horrors of my secret toils as I dabbled among the unhallowed damps of the grave or tortured the living animal to animate the lifeless clay?" (314–315).

9. What is important in this case is the way the life of the characters falls into Fleur's text: "Indeed, I wondered how you guessed that the butler locked me in the pantry to clean the silver, which he did indeed. Indeed he did. But Nanny on the rocking-horse, well, Nanny was a religious woman. On my rocking-horse with our butler, indeed, you know. It isn't the sort of thing Nanny would have done" (*LI* 43). The words seduce the "real" into them, through an inescapable attraction: "'My nanny was not actually evil,' murmured Sir Eric. 'In fact—' 'O, she was utterly evil,' Mrs Wilks said. 'I quite agree,' said Sir Quentin. 'She was plainly a sinister person.' . . . 'I will sleep on it,' said Sir Eric mildly" (*LI* 43–44).

10. See Roland Barthes, "The Death of the Author", and Maurice Blanchot, "The Work and the Death's Space", in *The Space of Literature*, 85-159.

3

Deadly Desires: The Inscription of the Body as Initiation into Narrative

"How like," says Lister, "the death wish is to the life-urge! How urgently does an overwhelming obsession with life lead to suicide! Really, it's best to be half-awake and half-aware. That is the happiest stage."
—Muriel Spark
Not to Disturb

Desire, death, and language are often closely associated, and it is this alliance in Muriel Spark's work that I shall examine in this chapter. Her texts draw attention to the way death becomes the locus of desire and discourse, how her characters share an erotic relationship with death, which gives the promise of a liberation from an imprisoning discourse and an initiation into what seems to be a new structure that opens up to a new beginning.

The relationship between desire and language is introduced by Freud through his description of the *Fort/Da* game of the child, which is a means of mastering the absence of the mother. It is this desire of the child for the mother that marks the individual's entrance into discourse, since it forces the child to control the mother's loss through language.

By trying, therefore, to master her absence, the child is involved in this continuous experiencing of absence and presence. It is through a form of death that this process is realized, since the child for the first time desires to envelop an absence within discourse, so that from a passive agent, s/he can take the place of the active subject and kill absence with language. However, there is a paradox in this effort, since the instrument through which the child tries to control absence—that is language—is "already a presence made of absence" (65) as

Lacan puts it in "Function and Field of Speech and Language." Therefore, instead of leading to control of loss, the word drives the individual to another loss, the loss of the signified before the signifier.

It is this paradox I intend to discuss in this chapter: how, in Muriel Spark's work, her characters and the narratives themselves are in a perpetual flight toward death, which they attempt to master through discourse but which always "hollows out" before them "the void toward which and from which [they] speak" (Foucault, "Language to Infinity" 53). Through its elevation into a supreme spectacle, the ultimate work of art, death can give the impression of a concrete object that can be imprisoned within the limits of the Symbolic Order and can give access to discourse. It is to death, therefore, that her characters turn in order to gain access to a discourse that will overpower all others. The "contradictory desire of narrative" that, according to Peter Brooks, is "driving toward the end which would be both its destruction and its meaning" (*Reading for the Plot* 58), in Muriel Spark is initiated from this end. The end—in the case I am discussing here, a death—is revealed almost at the beginning of her narratives, highlighting the destructive and constructive force of the desire for death in the text. In the novel *Territorial Rights*, a man is not only murdered by two women but his body is butchered in two and buried in the two sides of the women's garden, as I mentioned in the first chapter. This body is characteristically the corpus of narrative, since it initiates action in the novel. All characters and all plots inevitably revolve around this desecrated male body, which from its graves does not cease to inscribe those who turned it into an everlasting symbol of the power of desire.

These deadly desires are in direct association with the fabrication of a master plot in the narratives. Deaths become horrific spectacles, employed for the construction of plots that are going to dominate the text. The question of plot in Muriel Spark's work has been widely discussed, mainly by Ruth Whittaker in her work *The Faith and Fiction of Muriel Spark*. As Whittaker observes, "The subject of plot-making fascinates Mrs Spark: both the fictional construction of a novel and the scheming activities of her character. . . . In her novels the stress is either on the plots laid by her characters, or reflexively on a demonstration of how plot functions in a novel" (91).

In her fiction there are endless games with plots, as all the characters are involved in a process of "taking over," imprisoning others within the margins of their own constructs. Whittaker again states, "Besides revealing how a novelist constructs a plot, Mrs Spark's fiction contains a host of other manipulators: blackmailers, lawyers, film-directors, teachers, who may succumb to the temptation of imposing their plots on people in real life" (97). Muriel Spark is interested in revealing the syntax of the narratives—how this syntax works, how plots are constructed, and how they are used in order to imprison one another.[1]

In this chapter I endeavor to examine plottings and plotters in relation to narratives of death, which are very often closely associated with the question of the dominant voice in the narrative. Nothing can surpass the force of a violent and spectacular death, around which many of Spark's central scenes revolve. One witnesses a desire for the spectacle of death, which seduces with its promise of immortality, as it always marks the annihilation of the body and the character's entrance into language. Mastery of discourse, as I explained in the first chapter, is the main object of desire. As it can be achieved only through mastery of the spectacle of death, there seems to be a longing for these deadly narratives, which characters inflict upon themselves or upon others in order to secure the success of their plottings.

In *The Prime of Miss Jean Brodie*, where one plot is written over the other, the reader loses count of the deaths and resurrections. Miss Brodie is the first to teach her students this game; she makes her elect group part of her own body that she is trying to imprison within her discourse. The girls' images disappear behind her image and their minds are inserted in her own mind; she seeks utter domination through her fascist "education." She even causes the literal death of one of her girls whom she persuades to fight for Franco in Spain. However, this "body" of hers resists and rebels; Sandy betrays her and it is this betrayal that marks Jean Brodie's multiple deaths: the death of her life as a teacher, the death of her fictions, the death of her prime, and her literal death.[2] As we learn from the narrator, Jean Brodie dies of an "internal growth": "She had reckoned on her prime lasting till she was sixty. But this, the year after the war, was in fact Miss Brodie's last and fifty-sixth year. She looked older than that, she was suffering from an internal growth. This was her last year in the world and in another sense it was Sandy's" (*PMJB* 56). It is something from within the body itself that acquires a distorted form, expands, and destroys the whole. And Sandy—the part of Jean Brodie's body that has deconstructed, that has killed her cells—imposes an inscription on her own body, too. She imprisons it in the black garments of the nun and cages it behind the bars of her grill.

However, this is not the end of the novel. The end of the novel comes with Miss Brodie's resurrection. After the murder of the mother and the desire for the maternal body, Sandy enters an Order (Symbolic?), and the road to language is open. Quite significantly, it was the strict order of the school that could not tolerate the close connection between Miss Brodie and her students. In other words, the educational system forced Sandy to reject the Imaginary of Miss Brodie's world, and enter the Symbolic of the outside world. After this stage, Sandy is free to write and to resurrect Jean Brodie within her, but her desires are always annulled, postponed. The sense of lack is even more present in the end, after her entrance into the Symbolic Order of her transfiguration. Her passage from one stage to the other seems like an attempt to get hold of absence, the present absence of Miss Brodie after her death. Sandy behind her bars revives her teacher as the prime influence in her life. This is twice stated in the novel in the form of a short dialogue toward the beginning and at the end of the novel: "'What were the main influences of your school days, Sister Helena? Were they

literary or political or personal? Was it Calvinism?' Sandy said: 'There was a
Miss Jean Brodie in her prime'" (*PMJB* 127). It is Sandy's body now that is
suffering from an internal growth. The presence of Jean Brodie has grown to
such proportions within Sandy's body that it resists the imprisonment she has
forced on it and seeks to escape: "She clutched the bars of the grille as if she
wanted to escape from the dim parlour beyond, for she was not composed like
the other nuns who sat, when they received their rare visitors, well back in the
darkness with folded hands. But Sandy always leaned forward and peered,
clutching the bars with both hands, and the other sisters remarked it and said that
Sister Helena had too much to bear from the world" (*PMJB* 35). It is evident that
despite the murder of the mother figure, Sandy's entrance into this (Symbolic)
Order marks another death.

In Spark's work, deaths are very often constructed in a spectacular way and
are executed for the sheer pleasure of entering language and binding others'
plots in their powerful webs. The inscription of the body, according to Peter
Brooks, is inextricably bound to writing, signifying the "interplay of eros and
artistic creation" (*Body Work* 22). In Spark's novel *The Only Problem*, this idea
is foregrounded as Harvey Gotham's writing, closely related to *The Book of Job*
and the painting *Job Visited by His Wife* by Georges de la Tour, projects the
image of Job's wife on his wife Effie, who ends up dead, resembling the woman
in the painting more than ever before: "*L' Institut Médico-Légal* in Paris. Her
head was bound up, turban-wise, so that she looked more than ever like Job's
wife" (*OP* 186).[3] Harvey's eros is directed toward his wife through her
identification with the wife of Job in the painting, therefore killing her in her
resemblance to the dead signifier, long before Effie is actually murdered by the
police. Her dead body finally comes to foreground the unique union of death,
eros, and the work of art.

The desire for death, therefore, seems to be a desire for entrance into
discourse. You have to die before you can write. You kill and get killed, you
chase and are chased in a never ending process. Like Needle in "The Portobello
Road," who is killed by one of her childhood friends only to be resurrected and
haunt her murderer and her text with her ghostly presence, Spark's author-
characters are in a perpetual struggle for mastery of death, which is going to
bring with it the celebration of writing. Needle, unable to write about life while
living, manages to fulfill her one desire in life only after she dies. Death, then, is
a true liberation for her: "When I failed again and again to reproduce life in
some satisfactory and perfect form, I was the more imprisoned, for all my
carefree living, within my craving for this satisfaction" (PR 174). Needle, rather,
finds her voice after death. As Bronfen states in her work *Over Her Dead Body*:
"The privileged site of [the] connection [between language and the world] occurs
when the body loses its materiality in death" (54). Death is not the end for
Needle; it works as a new beginning, a symbolic transference to writing. It is
with death that she can at last enter this erotic relationship with the text, which

cannot be produced in life. This is the reason her "craving for this satisfaction"—in other words, for the satisfaction of inscribing—is displaced onto a desire for her death, since it is this death that will inevitably lead her to her text.

Even though Needle's death is not voluntary, there is an evident longing for this moment, which is going to liberate her writing powers and resurrect her into the Symbolic Order. It is as if her whole life is a driving toward this inscription that suddenly opens up the way to discourse. Her first-person narrative opens with her naming in the haystack:

One day in my young youth at high summer, lolling with my lovely companions upon a haystack, I found a needle. Already and privately for some years I had been guessing that I was set apart from the common run, but this of the needle attested the fact to my whole public: George, Kathleen and Skinny. I sucked my thumb, for when I had thrust my idle hand deep into the hay, the thumb was where the needle had stuck. . . . From that day I was known as Needle. (PR 7–8)

The beginning of this narrative not only inaugurates the story, it also marks Needle with the name and the blood that will be directly associated with her death, as is evident from the description of her murder, which I quoted in Chapter 1. It is this death that will in its turn initiate her into the narrative and place the absence of Needle within the realm of fiction. It is only through death that Needle can control the absence of language and return to "The Portobello Road" with the master plot of this absence, which overtakes all other plots. Following their first encounter after Needle's death in the Portobello Road, George is taken into a nursing home, where he confesses to Needle's murder, and then to Canada in order to be "well out of reach of the Portobello Road," but he never completely recovers.

This "self-inscription,"[4] then, is a writing of the body through which the individual acquires unique powers of mastery. The one who masters death is the one who constructs the master-plot, destroys all other fictions and dominates the narrative. In "Bang-bang You're Dead," the passage from the Imaginary into the Symbolic through death is more openly revealed as the reader follows the main character, Sybil, through the various stages of this process. The reader is introduced into the mirror stage in Sybil's life through a home movie from Africa, which for the first time introduces Sybil's double, Désirée. The names of the two women signify their striking difference and their mutual compatibility: Sybil, the "intellectual monster"—as she calls herself—the prophetess, the woman who possesses knowledge; Désirée, on the other hand, is a name that clearly signifies desire, the woman who is an object to be desired or longing for the desire of the male. In other words, this naming process works as a parody of the split of the woman into the intellect and the body, since the names of the two women are part of the process of conditioning them, assigning to them roles that they have to perform.

The words used to describe Désirée throughout the text are significant of her relationship with Sybil and her shadowlike existence. The first encounter of the two girls—perceived from Sybil's point of view—reads as follows:

"Look, there's a little girl rather like you, Sybil." Sybil, walking between her mother and father, one hand in each, had already craned round. The other child, likewise being walked along, had looked back too.

The other child wore a black velour hat turned up all round, a fawn coat of covert-coating, and at her neck a narrow white ermine tie. She wore white silk gloves. Sybil was dressed identically, and though this in itself was nothing to marvel at, . . . it did fortify the striking resemblance in features, build, and height, between the two children. Sybil suddenly felt she was walking past her own reflection in the long looking-glass. There was her peak chin, her black bobbed hair under her hat, with its fringe almost touching her eyebrows. Her wide-spaced eyes, her nose very small like a cat's. (BYD 79)

When Sybil is in Africa one of her friends tells her: "I met a girl last night, it was funny. I thought it was you at first and called over to her. But she wasn't really like you close up, it was just an *impression*" (BYD 91–92, italics added). The word "impression" here could be applied to Désirée, thus emphasizing her immateriality and the fact that she is made in the image of Sybil. Moreover, it is in the dark moments of the day, when the sun sets and the long shadows fall that she looks like Sybil. Désirée's husband tells Sybil after his wife's death: "'In some ways you *do* look a little bit like Désirée. . . . In some lights'" (BYD 110). As Otto Rank states in his book *The Double*: "[A]mong the very first and most primitive concepts of the soul is that of the shadow, which appears as a faithful image of the body but of a lighter substance. . . . primitive man considers his shadow as something real, as being attached to him" (82–83). Désirée is attached to Sybil and follows her everywhere while Sybil is attracted to her as to a magnet.

The battle between these two women or, should I say, these two images of the same woman, starts from the beginning of their lives together, when they take part in shooting affairs, where the men hand them the guns and make the rules. The first game that the two girls play is a game of life and death, introduced by two boys, the Dobels, in which "Désirée continually shot Sybil dead, contrary to the rules, whenever she felt like it [while] Sybil resented with the utmost passion the repeated daily massacre of herself before the time was ripe" (BYD 82). Désirée, as the very first reflection of herself that Sybil encounters, exerts a peculiar attraction to Sybil, who, as though through an inevitable compulsion to repeat,[5] cannot escape going to her and experiencing this fictional death without actually dying.[6]

I shall refuse to be dead, Sybil promised herself. I'll break the rule. If it doesn't count with her why should it count with me? I won't roll over any more when she bangs you're dead to me. Next time, tomorrow if it isn't raining. . . .

But Sybil simply did roll over. When John and Hugh Dobell called out to her that Désirée's bang-bang did not count she started hopefully to resurrect herself; but "It does count, it *does*. That's the rule," Désirée counter-screeched. And Sybil dropped back flat, knowing utterly that this was final. (BYD 83)

The two girls seem to be in a constant duel in this spectacular game, where the normal image of the "stupid" woman has to kill her double who, because her "intelligence [is] superior to [the boys']" (BYD 83), consequently poses a threat to the established order. Only Sybil/Sibylla, as I mentioned in the second chapter, never dies.

This game of life and death is repeated as a playact with the Westons, Désirée, and her husband Barry. Sybil, now a grown woman, goes repeatedly to the Westons to kill herself by assuming another personality in a performance that the Westons direct. Although Sybil strongly resented this game, "she went in obedience to them. The Westons were a magnetic field" (BYD 94): "It was like a game for three players. According to the rules, she was to be in love, unconsciously, with Barry, and tortured by the contemplation of Désirée's married bliss" (BYD 98).

What is this magnetic field that always leads women to their (self-) destruction in Spark's work? It seems like a desire on the part of Sybil to overcome her longing for the text, in a recognition of the Other's imaginary unity of her "married bliss." Therefore, she surrenders to these series of deaths that may open the way to mastery of her multiple desires and a subsequent "normalization" when her longing for the text is replaced by sexual desire. Sybil "engaged in [sexual relationships] as an act of virtue done against the grain, and for a brief time [they] . . . absolved her from the reproach of her sexlessness" (BYD 105) which she considers abnormal. Her body is not hers; it belongs to the language and the culture that condition the rules under which it must function, held captive by the multiple deaths it must go through in order to be immersed in dominant culture. Her body belongs to her shadow, her double Désirée—a male construct—and she cannot have it back.

It is as if an abstract Law leads Sybil to marry a man that she finds is "becoming a bore" (BYD 86) eighteen months after their marriage. Although she is bored by sex, when her husband dies she has three affairs in an attempt "to do the normal thing. Perhaps I may try again. Perhaps, if I should meet the right man" (BYD 91). Sybil seems to be repelled by this game with "normalities" but she constantly returns to it in order to be killed over and over again. She is unable to escape the death of these patriarchal structures that inscribe her body into particular behavior patterns. Critics have pointed out that all these notions of normality and abnormality have been imposed on women, who seem unable to escape them. As Philip Martin explains in his book *Mad Women in Romantic Writing*, "Hippocratic medical writings . . . recommended regular sexual intercourse (or pregnancy) as a cure for hysteria," and sexual abstinence is considered "as a prime cause for woman's disorder and derangement" (16).

According to this mythology, a woman must have sex, otherwise she will go mad. The realization that this discourse, which has been imposed on her, is totally alienated from the reality of her experience, is perhaps the reason why Sybil "at the idea 'right man' . . . felt a sense of intolerable desolation and could not stop shivering" (BYD 91).

It is this same discourse that conditions Needle, an ambitious woman "set apart from the common run" (PR 164) as she believes, who does not want to get married but whose "ambition [is] to write about life, which first I had to see" (PR 168). However, she complies with the dominant idea of marriage as a way to solve her financial problems: "I got engaged to Skinny, but shortly after that I was left a small legacy . . . . This somehow decided me that I didn't love Skinny so I gave him back the ring" (PR 169). Or it is a means to "see" life: "[T]he main attraction of marrying Skinny was his prospective expeditions to Mesopotamia" (PR 179). In other words, Needle, although she seems willing to conform to patriarchal conventions is enabled in a stroke of luck to rebel and become a very independent and self-fulfilled person in whose life men do not play the central role. As such, she poses a threat to what Kristeva calls "the realm of the proper, culture, [which] functions . . . by man's classic fear of seeing himself expropriated, seeing himself deprived . . . by his refusal to be deprived" (486). Needle has to be sacrificed by George, who seems to stand for "the realm of the proper" in the story, in order for the threat of the expropriation of the male to cease to exist. As it was evident from her framing in the beginning, George's text has arranged her ending: she is to be the victim of a sacrifice.

In the same way, Sybil's sexual desires seem to be replaced by the desire for the text, which becomes dominant only when her body is weak. It is only at these moments that Sybil manages to overpower her body and "write" her affairs away: "Sybil had three affairs in the space of two years, to put herself to the test. . . . The affairs ended when she succumbed to one of her attacks of tropical 'flu, and lay in a twilight of the senses on a bed which had been set on the stone stoep and overhung with a white mosquito net like something bridal. With damp shaky hands she would write a final letter to the man and give it to her half-caste maid to post" (BYD 90).

In order, then, to escape this imprisonment, both Needle and Sybil in a sense provoke their deaths, which will mark their liberation and their entrance into another form of discourse. Sybil's rejection of her ex-boyfriend's marriage proposal and his art is a decisive step toward her "murder": "David forced his way into the house. Sybil was alarmed. None of her previous lovers had persisted in this way. 'It's your duty to marry me.' 'Really, what next?' 'It's your duty to me as a man and a poet.' She did not like his eyes. 'As a poet,' she said, 'I think you're a third-rater'" (BYD 105). Once more Sybil flees toward her murder, another paradox in Spark's fiction, since it is finally not *her* murder, but the murder of the Other, the murder of Désirée/Desire, which appears to liberate

Sybil and allows her finally to resolve her conflicts and to embrace her narratives:

Sybil was feeling disturbed by David's presence in the place. . . . Thinking of his sullen staring at her on the lawn, she felt he might make a scene. She heard a gasp from the dining-room behind her.

She looked round, but in the same second it was over. A deafening crack from the pistol and Désirée crumpled up. A movement by the inner door and David held the gun to his head. Sybil screamed, and was aware of running footsteps upstairs. The gun exploded again and David's body dropped sideways. (BYD 109)

It is a similar force that drives Needle to her murder by her friend George. She had evidently been driving toward it from the beginning of the story, because of her naming and her conditioning by the "needle in the haystack" episode but also because of her longing, her incessant desire for entrance into the realm of fiction. So, when George gives her the opportunity to escape death she rejects it, thus complying to, or even inciting, her death:

"You'll keep my secret, won't you? You promised." He had released my feet. I edged a little further from him.

I said, "If Kathleen intends to marry you, I shall tell her that you're already married."

"You wouldn't do a dirty trick like that, Needle? You're going to be happy with Skinny, you wouldn't stand in the way of my—'"

"I must, Kathleen's my best friend," I said swiftly.

He looked as if he would murder me and he did. (PR 29)

THE SPECTACLE OF THANATOS: A CASE

> Dying
> Is an art, like everything else
> I do it exceptionally well.
>
> I do it so it feels like hell.
> I do it so it feels real.
> I guess you could say I've a call.
> —Sylvia Plath
> "Lady Lazarus"

In Spark's deadly narratives, the life force and the death instinct intermingle and explode into each other. Eros and Thanatos cease to be two opposing forces, and instead work together to unleash hidden desires. As Marcuse argued, "The uncontrolled Eros is just as fatal as his deadly counterpart, the death instinct" (11), especially in the practice of perversions, where we witness a "fusion [of Eros and the death instinct which] makes manifest the erotic component in the death instinct and the fatal component in the sex instinct" (46). The more spectacular the act, the more intense is the feeling that death marks the entrance into discourse, that death is discourse in the same way that discourse is death.

Lise, in *The Driver's Seat*, is characterized by her desire for absence, and she embarks on a journey toward the final appeasement of her demand—the spectacular death that is going to fill the gap, satiate the lack. The paradox in the relationship between desire, death, and language reaches its peak in this novella, since it is literal death/absence that is Lise's locus of desire and discourse. The novella depicts Lise's effort to master the absence of her life with death, which will eventually initiate the narrative. The narrative, then, depends for its completion and also its initiation on the end that Lise desires.

Her death is an act of extreme liberation, almost a task that has to be achieved in order to secure entrance into discourse. Maurice Blanchot in *The Space of Literature* underlines:

Death, in the human perspective, is not a given, it must be achieved. It is a task, one which we take up actively, one which becomes the source of our activity and mastery. Man dies, that is nothing. But man *is*, starting from his death. He ties himself tight to his death with a tie of which he is the judge. He makes his death; he makes himself mortal and in this way gives himself the power of a maker and gives to what he makes its meaning and its truth. The decision to be without being is possibility itself: the possibility of death. (96)

It is her death that initiates the narrative of the novella; it is because of her death that Lise enters the realm of fiction. Lise's absence becomes a work of art, an impressive spectacle that is worth special attention. It is a unique moment in Spark's work, where all dichotomies are at the same time celebrated and violated.

In this novella, the female protagonist, Lise, enveloped within others' narratives, immersed in a perpetually absent presence, suddenly unleashes her desires and becomes so enamored with the narcissistic image of her dead body that she complies to the writing of her self into the ultimate spectacle of death. "The driver's seat" and Lise's preoccupation with her death could be taken as a realisation of Zarathustra's advice: "[E]veryone who wants glory must take leave of honour in good time and practise the difficult art of—going at the right time. . . . For many a man, life is a failure; a poison-worm eats at his heart. So let him see to it that his death is all the more a success" (Nietzsche, *Thus Spoke Zarathustra* 98). "Having death within reach, docile and reliable," according to Blanchot "makes life possible, for it is exactly what provides air, space, free and joyful movement: it is possibility" (97). Lise's decision to seize this possibility, to master the spectacle of her murder—which she will stage—is a form of realisation of her desire for the control over her own body that has been denied her. As Kirilov says: "I will kill myself to affirm my insubordination, my new and terrifying liberty" (as quoted in Blanchot, *The Space of Literature* 97).

In her case it is not the simple "interplay of eros and artistic creation" that Brooks referred to in his work (*Body Work* 22), but the interplay of eros and death, a death that is elevated to a work of art.

Lise perceives her violent murder as the only escape, her only way out from a dead life, enclosed as it is in a coffinlike pinewood flat, which looks "as if it were uninhabited" (*DS* 15). The writing of her murder gives her the power to escape imprisonment and, what is more, to surpass the rules that the writings of others have imposed upon her, to experience the liberation of new voices and new images, apart from those of the spinster she has been conditioned to play. Her course toward the spectacle of Thanatos runs parallel to a course through a series of voices and images that are going to mark her after-death image, as a sort of revenge against any form of structure that imposes a logos more silent than silence itself.

It is evident, then, that Lise is after an image, her own image in death, that is going to give her access to discourse from which she has been excluded. She doesn't kill the self, she kills her image, as Blanchot points out in *The Space of Literature*:

The expression "I kill myself" suggests the doubling which is not taken into account. For "I" is a self in the plenitude of its action and resolution, capable of acting sovereignly upon itself, always strong enough to reach itself with its blow. And yet the one who is thus struck is no longer I, but another, so that when I kill myself, perhaps it is "I" who does the killing, but it is not done to me. Nor is it my death—the one I dealt—that I have now to die, but rather the death which I refused, which I neglected, and which is this very negligence—perpetual flight and inertia. (Blanchot, *The Space of Literature* 107)

Lise, from the beginning of the narrative, sets out to write the fictional death of her image—the spectacle of the Other, whose murder gives her the opportunity, for the first time, to sit in "the driver's seat," to "write" her own destiny, to escape her anonymity by entering her own narrative. Her identity disappears with her passport, which she stuffs in the backseat of a taxi, ridding her self of the image of the woman, "whose lips are usually pressed together with the daily disapprovals of the accountants' office where she worked continually" (*DS* 9). It is her wish to experience this Otherness that leads Lise to her self-sacrifice in an effort to sit in "the driver's seat." She is a woman imprisoned in the imposed loneliness of her "spinsterhood," that is so nightmarishly portrayed in the coffinlike emptiness of her flat, with its "fixed" and "stackable" furniture that "fold[s] away into the dignity of unvarnished pinewood" (*DS* 14).[7]

Wearing distorted masks and with her lips now always "slightly parted," she enters a proliferation of images, voices, words, and languages,[8] playing various roles—the secretary, the teacher, the widow, the intellectual, the street prostitute, the sacrificial victim, the raped and murdered woman in a park—that have been attributed to women, feeling perhaps the catharsis of this ritual seeping through her body. The psychedelic proliferation of the colors of her clothes—a dress with a "lemon-yellow top with a skirt patterned in bright V's of orange, mauve and blue," "a summer coat with narrow stripes, red and white, with a white collar" (*DS* 10–11)—which mark out her body as ex-centric, matches the multitude of masks that she wears in her desire to disrupt, disorient, and disturb. In pursuit of the female voice that will render her invincible, she kills her imposed spinster self, thus symbolically killing what Irigaray calls the "bod[y] . . . encoded within a system" (*This Sex Which Is Not One* 206). At the check-in desk at the airport, where she begins her journey toward the land of her death, she speaks in a voice different from her normal voice, "in a little-girl tone which presumably is taken by those within hearing to be her normal voice even if a nasty one" (*DS* 19), playing the role of the woman who never grew up. Later she speaks a "foreignly accented English" (*DS* 22), pretending to be a tourist going on holiday "look[ing] for a gay time" (*DS* 23). At some point when she is already at her destination, she plays the role of a widowed teacher from Iowa, New Jersey, "a temptress in the old-fashioned style" (*DS* 78), "an . . . exotic, intellectual, . . . treasure" (*DS* 79).[9] She speaks all these different voices as if she is all women in one, speaking for all womanhood. She becomes the all-encompassing image of Otherness in a narrative that does not belong to her but which she intends to make hers.

She is fascinated by her own death, the figure of her dead body in the park, and as she "cannot make of death an object of will," Lise shows, characteristically, in Blanchot's view, an enormous "love for details, the patient, maniacal concern for the utmost mediocre realities" (105). As Blanchot further explains in the *Space of Literature*:

One cannot "plan" to kill oneself. One prepares to do so, one acts in view of the ultimate gesture which still belongs to the normal category of things to do, but this gesture does not have death in view, it does not look at death, it does not keep death before it. Hence the attention to minutiae often symptomatic in those who are about to die—the love for details, the patient, maniacal concern for the most mediocre realities. . . . you don't *want* to die, you cannot make death an object of will. . . . Whoever wants to die can only want the borders of death, the utilitarian death which is in the world and which one reaches through the precision of a workman's tools. Whoever wants to die does not die, he loses the will to die. He enters the nocturnal realm of fascination wherein he dies in a passion bereft of will. (104–105)

Lise becomes enamored with this image, a strange case of narcissistic necrophilia that marks her desire for a beautiful death, where the beauty of body in death acquires an enormous significance, a significance that it used to have for the male heroes of Homer, where the hero would not be allowed to rest if his body did not retain its beauty in death.

From very early in the novella, it becomes apparent that Lise's seduction by her image reaches the heights of a sexual excitation: "Lise does not appear to listen. She studies herself. This way and that, in the mirror of the fitting room.

She lets the coat hang over the dress. Her lips part, and her eyes narrow; she breathes for a moment as in a trance" (*DS* 11). Like another Narcissus, vainly desiring his image in the water and dying because of this desire, Lise perceives this destiny as the only true satisfaction of her desire.

Still, the text alienates her by trapping her, not only in the image of the spinster but also in the image of the mad Other, which is revealed by facts about her life the narrative is trying to hide, re-presenting the attitude of society toward madness, since, according to Phyllis Chesler, "madness is shut away from sight, shamed, brutalized, denied, and feared" (26). In the beginning, we learn that she has worked in an accountant's office for eighteen years continually "except for the months of illness" (*DS* 9). The cause of this illness is implied when she suffers a crisis "of laughing and . . . crying all in a flood," which "conveyed to her that she had done again what she had not done for five years" (*DS* 9–10). But where was she during those months of absence? The answer is given when she asks her murderer, a man who has been treated for psychological problems, about the clinic where he had his treatment: "'Were the walls of the clinic pale green in all the rooms? Was there a great big tough man in the dormitory at night, patrolling up and down every so often, just in case?' 'Yes,' he says. 'Stop trembling,' she says. 'It's the madhouse tremble'" (*DS* 102).

She knows the "madhouse," as she calls it, very well. This intimacy of knowledge sheds light on her suicide attempt. It is her wish to escape the confines of her limited existence that leads Lise to identify, through her self-sacrificial act, with the female heroines who were led to their self-sacrifices—from ancient tragic mythic figures, like Iphigenia, Macaria, Antigone, Polyxena to the exceptional case of Joan of Arc "the only Persephone-Kore Maiden in modern history who is not raped or impregnated by her father" as Phyllis Chesler explains. Lise's self-sacrificial act makes her part of this long tradition of women who are murdered for the preservation of male culture. She desires the death of her body in order to preserve the life of her image.

Lise is entangled in a vicious circle of fictionality, where the reader is never allowed to feel the reassuring certainty of a reality. As Patricia Waugh states in her work *Metafiction*, the characters in Muriel Spark's fiction are "trapped within language itself, within an arbitrary system of signification which appears to offer no means of escape" (120). The spectacle of death seems to offer a means of escape for Spark's characters as it grants them entrance into the realm of the Symbolic.

Lise—like Frederick Christopher in *The Public Image*, to whose death I shall refer in the next chapter—is trying to find Logos in silence (Thanatos). For her, the word is not in the beginning but in the end, or rather the end is a new beginning, a beginning that will take her out of the silence of her existence. Blanchot observes that:

The weakness of suicide lies in the fact that whoever commits it is still too strong. He is demonstrating a strength suitable only for a citizen of the world. Whoever kills himself could, then, go on living: whoever kills himself is linked to hope, the hope of finishing it all, and hope reveals his desire to begin, to find the beginning again in the end, to inaugurate in that ending a meaning which, however, he means to challenge by dying. (*The Space of Literature* 103)

Lise seems to be writing—or perhaps complying with the writing of—her own text of self-destruction, so we have no deceptions of a possible escape. In Lise's narrative, we are aware of a very restricted structure that cannot be broken. The spectacular ritual of the sacrifice is conducted by the victim herself. She is the power that attracts and seduces her victims with the void around her, the death smell that she emits. Her murderer, like the vultures, is attracted to the body that is about to die, but this time the body takes the vulture with it into the void.

Lise, who appears to be playing the role of the priestess in control of the ritual, "walks up to the great windows of the Pavilion"—the place of her sacrifice—"and presses to look inside" (*DS* 105), as if wanting to penetrate the mystery. The two—Lise and her murderer—approach the altar and the ritual begins: "She *says*, 'I'm going to lie down here. *Then* you tie my hands with my scarf; I'll put one wrist over the other, it's the *proper* way. *Then* you'll tie my ankles together with your necktie. *Then* you strike.' She points *first* to her throat. '*First* here,' she *says*. *Then*, pointing to a place beneath each breast, she *says*, '*Then* here and here. *Then* anywhere you like'" (*DS* 105–106, italics added). The words "first" and "then"—the latter is repeated six times in this short excerpt—imply that she has a specific process in her mind that must be followed without deviation. Everything must be done "the proper way," like the sacrificial rituals in ancient tragedies. It seems that any violation of this procedure is going to desecrate the act.

However, the signs that she uses to communicate the meaning of her sacrifice are all taken from the dominant culture. Although she may have escaped the confines of her room, she has not managed to escape male culture.[10] But all these signs are at once celebrated and violated. The stabs on Lise's body will have the shape of the cross (one stab on her throat and one under each breast), a symbol she used before, when "she [put] a little cross beside one of the small pictures which [was] described on the map as 'The Pavilion'" (*DS* 49), in order to determine the place where her murder was going to take place. The cross, as symbol of "perpetual renovation and cosmic regeneration, of universal fecundity and of sanctity, of absolute reality and, in the final reckoning, of immortality" (Eliade, *Myths, Rites, Symbols* 454), emerges to relate this act of self-sacrifice—which comes from an anonymous woman—to the eternity of Christ's crucifixion and the eternity of the symbolism of the Tree of Life.

However, the cross is in fact the most important symbol of a male-dominated religion, of a male god that has replaced the female goddess of fertility and has brought a new order to the world. It also associates Lise again with Joan of Arc, whose sacrifice, although she was a leader of men, served "the purposes of male renewal" (26) as Phyllis Chesler states.[11] Even the weapon that she uses, a paper knife, is clearly an emblem of male domination; the knife symbolizes the penis, the symbol of male desire that has eliminated female desire, but since it is a knife for paper, it also stands for the pen that writes women and kills them into artistic objects. All this gives further emphasis to the fact that she hands this weapon, that literally and metaphorically kills her, to her murderer:

She takes the paper-knife from its sheath, feels the edge and the point, and says that it isn't very sharp but it will do. "Don't forget," she says, "that it's curved." She looks at the engraved sheath in her hand and lets it fall carelessly from her fingers. "After you've stabbed," she says, "be sure to twist it upwards or it may not penetrate far enough." She demonstrates the movement with her wrist. . . . Then she lies down on the gravel and he grabs at the knife.

"Tie my hands first," she says, crossing her wrists. "Tie them with the scarf."

He ties her hands, and she tells him in a sharp, quick voice to take off his necktie and bind her ankles.

"No," he says, kneeling over her, "not your ankles."

"I don't want any sex," she shouts. "You can have it afterwards. Tie my feet and kill, that's all. They will come and sweep it up in the morning."

All the same, he plunges into her, with the knife poised high.

"Kill me," she says, and repeats it in four languages.

As the knife descends to her throat she screams, evidently perceiving how final is finality. She screams and then her throat gurgles while he stabs with a turn of his wrist exactly as she instructed. Then he stabs wherever he likes and stands up, staring at what he has done. (*DS* 106–107)

In this ritual we seem to have a set of oppositions or doubles: man/woman, activity/passivity, sadism/masochism. The roles have changed now and the murderer plays the active part of the sadist who inflicts pain and kills the passive woman, the masochist, who desires the pain and her death.[12] As Freud states in his work "Instincts and Their Vicissitudes," the *"reversal of an instinct into its opposite* resolves . . . into two different processes: a *change* from *activity to passivity*, and a *reversal of its content"* (*On Metapsychology* 124).

The most important moment of male domination comes with the ambiguous sexual violation of the woman, which coincides with the moment of killing. In an extreme case of homicide, Lise, the victim, "speaks" her murder and her murderer, who is deprived of his rightful place as the victor in the scene. Author and character, victor and victim, death and life, silence and logos are all intermingled at this moment, where all structures are, at the same time, glorified and ridiculed.

Lise's disinterest in or disinclination for sex has been suggested repeatedly in the narrative to this point. As she says: "[Sex] is all right at the time and it's all right before, . . . but the problem is afterwards. That is, if you aren't just an animal. Most of the time, afterwards it's pretty sad" (*DS* 103). After the union of the two bodies her usual loneliness is further reinforced. Lise often asserts her disgust for sex in her course toward her death: "'I don't want sex with you. I'm not interested in sex. I've got other interests and as a matter of fact I've got something on my mind that's got to be done'" (*DS* 80), or "'I have no time for sex. . . . Sex is no use to me, I assure you'" (*DS* 94). Her desire to avoid any context in her relationships with men could also indicate her fear that sex would interfere with her death and destroy the power of her spectacle.

Her desire for sex is displaced by a desire for death, as I stated earlier. Lise seems to be narcissistically preoccupied with the image of her body.[13] As Kristeva states in her work *Tales of Love,* "[Narcissus] Loves, he loves Himself—active and passive, subject *and* object. Actually, Narcissus is not completely without object. *The object of Narcissus is psychic space; it is representation itself, fantasy*" (116). It is this love of the image that leads Lise to the construction of her narrative and the integration of herself as subject and object of her narration—in short, her self-sacrifice. This narrative has a lot in common with the modern novel which, as Linda Hutcheon states in her book *Narcissistic Narrative,* resembles the myth of Narcissus in its highly self-reflective quality, "ceaselessly regarding . . . its formal beauties" (14). The reader is aware of the process of construction of her text that alienates him/her and does not allow his/her immersion in the false reality of the plot. However, as Kristeva further comments, "Narcissus in love hides the suicidal Narcissus; the most urgent of all drives is the death drive. Left to itself, without the assistance of projection upon the other, the Ego takes itself for a preferential target of aggression and murder" (124). As Narcissus's self-love led him to his self-destruction, so Lise, lacking any other object on which to project her Ego, projects her aggressive instincts onto herself and is led to the construction of her self-imposed death.

The ambiguity of the scene of the crime is highly significant. As Burkert states in his book *Homo Necans,* "[S]exuality is always intimately involved in ritual" (58) and "[M]ale aggression and male sexuality are closely bound up with one another, stimulated simultaneously and almost always inhibited together" (59). The moment of killing sexually arouses the murderer: the verb "plunge" entails some rush and violence, and the image of the "knife poised high," the weapon ready to hit and kill, clearly symbolizes the erect penis—which according to Jane Gallop "contrary to the symbolic veiled phallus, is not monolithic power, but desire, need for another body" (*The Daughter's Seduction* 100)—that will enter the female body and kill it by raping it. The final moment of penetration in the murder, when the murderer "plunges into her, with the knife poised high" (*DS* 106), emphasizes the disruption of all dichotomies. The bodies of man and woman, murderer and victim respectively—or vice versa—seduce each other into a union of love and hatred, soon to be divided or united by the knife that is going to penetrate, like the penis that penetrated before it. It is actually a moment of interpenetration, with Lise entering the male body with her tongue and the man piercing her with the penknife and his penis.[14] The moment of union of the bodies—that also seems like a terrible moment of separation, since Lise has desperately tried to avoid it—dissolves into death, as Lise crosses the boundary and is forever placed outside narrative. This moment of the inside-outside, union and separation, finally seduces Lise into an absence that marks her entrance into art.

Lise is not the only woman in Spark's works who is raped. Needle in "The Portobello Road" also experiences the same sexual violation and this scene is similarly ambivalent, coinciding with her murder. The way this sacrifice is presented by the victim, Needle, is highly significant. The man, as the stronger sex, is over the woman, "kneeling on her body to keep it still." Although she is struggling to get free, the male is so much stronger that her efforts fail. We get the impression of a "giant of a man" (PR 166) who is holding "both [the woman's] wrists in his huge hand" and a tiny woman who is unable to escape his grasp.

The analogy between the act of sacrifice and the violent penetration of the female body appears again at the close of the murder scene. The dead body of the woman, which George is trying to hide by pushing it "into the stack, as he ma[kes] a deep nest for [it], tearing up the hay to make a groove for it the length of the corpse, and finally pulling the warm dry stuff in a mound over this concealment" (PR 185), seems to work as a phallic symbol that plunges into the vagina, the haystack. The words "deep" and "groove" reinforce this idea of penetration. However, the diction of this sentence gives us the impression of an enforced intrusion: the phrasal verb "tear up" entails violence in the effort of the body to penetrate the hay, and the word "dry" along with the whole image of the dryness of the haystack reinforces this feeling of violence. The woman's body is used as a phallic symbol after her violent death by the beastlike man who is thirsty for the female blood and body. Needle's last impression of George is highly significant: "I saw the red full lines of his mouth and the white slit of his teeth last thing on earth" (PR 185). The fullness and the red color of the mouth are an image of sexuality, but together with the white teeth, they are also an image of bestiality. From the beginning of the text George, with "his enormous mouth, the bright, sensuous lips, the large brown eyes forever brimming with pathos" (PR 166), seemed to resemble the big beast that would devour the little girl.

After the violation of the bodies of these women we get the impression that the men are in control of the situation. In *The Driver's Seat*, after the man has stabbed "he stands up, staring at what he has done" (*DS* 107), and in "The Portobello Road," "George climbed down, took up his bottle of milk, and went his way" (PR 185) after strangling the woman. According to Bronfen: "Horror at the sight of death turns into satisfaction, since the survivor is not himself dead. The dead body is in the passive, horizontal position, cut down, fallen, while the survivor stands erect, imbued with a feeling of superiority. By implication the corpse is feminine, the survivor masculine" (65). The man is now in control—or is he?

There is much to suggest that the man is not as much in control as we might think. Lise is complicitous with male discourse up to a point. If we examine her art more closely we will find, along with the male symbols, a cluster of female symbols as well: the fact that she does not want a stain-resisting dress but chooses one that will show the stains of blood proves her close relationship with blood. It is Susan Gubar who points out the "centrality of blood as a symbol furnished by the female body" ("The Blank Page" 253) and thinks that "the woman artist who experiences herself as killed into art may also experience herself as bleeding into print" (248). It is Lise's blood that prints her image "in the newspapers of four languages" (*DS* 18).

Lise is the one who in fact "writes" her body; she uses it in order to leave a sign of her presence behind her, "successfully [to register] the fact of her presence . . . among the . . . thousands" (*DS* 20). Lise's journey toward the construction of her deathly narrative is an effort to experience herself as Other. As Bronfen suggests: "[S]uicide implies an authorship with one's own life, a form of writing the self and writing death that is ambivalently poised between self-construction and self-destruction: a confirmation that is also an annihilation of the self, and as such another kind of attempt to know the self as radically different and other from the consciously known self during life" (142). Her suicidal narrative will enable the author to experience herself as the object of narration, the Other of her text. The fact that it is she who directs the ritual, the one who gives the orders and manipulates the man, whom she reduces to the object of the narrative and traps into the confines of her text, indicates that the roles have changed again: after he kills her "he stands staring for a while and then, he hesitates as if he had forgotten something of her bidding. Suddenly he wrenches off his necktie and bends to tie her ankles together with it. He runs to the car, taking his chance and knowing that he will at last be taken" (*DS* 107).

The fact that the man is now the other, the absence in the text, because Lise has reduced him to that minor role, becomes evident when she is asked how she will know that she has found the right man: "'Will you feel a *presence*? Is that how you'll know?' 'Not really a presence,' Lise says. 'The *lack* of an absence, that's what *it* is. I know I'll find *it*'" (*DS* 71, italics added). The man is deprived of his name, of his presence, of his existence as a "he"; he is eliminated and trapped in a nonexistence, an "it," to the Lacanian Lack that is always identified with the woman. He is drawn to her as the victim is drawn to the hidden panther by his irresistible scent.[15] As Baudrillard comments: "[I]n a strategy (?) of seduction one draws the other into one's area of weakness. A calculated weakness, an incalculable weakness: one challenges the other to be taken in. A weakness of failure: isn't the panther's scent itself a weakness, an abyss which the other animals approach giddily? In fact, the panther of the mythical scent is simply the epicenter of death, and from this weakness subtle fragrances emerge"

(*Seduction* 83). Lise not only seduces her victim and victor to her, she moreover writes him through her words. She tells him "[Y]ou're a sex maniac" (*DS* 103), thus framing him, placing him in a text that he cannot avoid; as he later confesses to the police: "'She told me to kill her and I killed her. . . . she was telling me to kill her all the time. She told me precisely what to do'" (*DS* 107).

If she "speaks" her alienated body through the process and the act of her death, it may become hers. In the same way, if she experiments with the different male discourses that have been assigned to women, if she speaks and distorts them all, she may make them hers. When the man tells her that "a lot of women get killed in the park," she adopts popular masculine myths of rape and insists that "it's because they want to be," "they look for it" (*DS* 104). The powerful force in the narrative, the constructor of language, Lise eliminates the feminine character in order to produce, or rather to ironically heighten a stereotype of women. After speaking this myth, she goes on to play it out, thus "seiz[ing] it . . . [and] mak[ing] it hers."

The man runs away from the scene of the crime after the murder, but: "He sees already the gleaming buttons of the policemen's uniforms, hears the cold and the confiding, the hot and the barking voices, sees already the holsters and epaulets and all those trappings that are devised to protect them from the indecent exposure of fear and pity, pity and fear" (*DS* 107). "Fear and pity, pity and fear," this echo of Aristotle's definition of tragedy,[16] used at the end of the novel, could associate Lise's narrative with ancient Greek tragedy. The fact that she chooses tragedy—which has always been associated with male writers—as her genre, is significant of her effort to subvert the order. She, an anonymous woman, sets out "with absolute purpose" (*DS* 8) to construct a tragedy, and she disrupts its rules since "pity and fear" are denied the reader or the spectator. The police are protected from it by "the holsters and epaulets." Also the narrator, who assumes "the position of the aesthetically involved spectator, distanced, disinterested, treating the representation of the dying body only as a signifier pointing to many other signifiers" (Bronfen 45) "transfigur[es] [this] natural event into a sign spectacle" (Kellner 107), and Lise, who "embraces certain forms of sign culture and pays less and less attention to materiality (needs, desire, suffering)" (Kellner 107–108), deprives the reader of his/her right to pity and fear.

The question at the end is what remains for her after the climax of her narrative, the sacrificial scene? "As the knife descends to her throat she screams, evidently perceiving how final is finality" (*DS* 106–107). The repetition of the word "final" leaves no hope for a continuation; this is the end for Lise. Similar to the narcissistic process from self-love to self-destruction that she followed, her text followed a process of preoccupation with its formal structures, and by revealing them, it destroyed its own essence, its false reality, like the literature of the sixties and seventies which, as Linda Hutcheon believes, "seemed to many . . . to have been playing with its own destruction" (*Narcissistic Narrative* 15).

Lise's narrative will also be killed by the objective, male narrator who takes over after her murder, indicating that others will appropriate her image; it will become male property through the media that will continue to kill the image of the anonymous woman who caused her own death in a park somewhere in the south, killing in this way fiction into fact, representation into reality.

Lise's desire for the image of the dead body is not satiated. The intervention of the narrator deprives her of her *jouissance*, and makes her desire for the body-text ever more distant and false, transferring it to the realm of the uncanny. Her desire is similar to "the contradictory desire of narrative" that Peter Brooks mentions: "driving toward the end which would be both its destruction and its meaning, suspended on the metonymic rails which tend toward that end without ever being able quite to say the terminus" (*Reading for the Plot* 58).

Quite significantly, the texts in the end actually reinstate the endless game of language, desire, and death. Sybil is once again found at the mirror stage, where she is again before her double—both Désirée and her image in the reel—which she tries to manipulate through language, through her commentary to the viewers of the video, which further stresses her alienation. The end of the narrative finds her still wondering: "[A]m I a woman, she thought calmly, or an intellectual monster? She was so accustomed to this question within herself that it needed no answer" (BYD 111).

In Needle's case her liberation after her death is not fully accomplished either. She does not completely control her voice, since there is some other being, another "author," that controls the whole text and Needle: "It was not for me to speak to Kathleen, but I had a sudden inspiration which caused me to say quietly, 'Hallo, George'" (PR 166). She is not the master of her voice; the other "author" controls her speech by allowing her to speak to whoever He chooses. Thus, she is again manipulated by another Law, a permanent one because this time there is no death to liberate her.

For Muriel Spark's women, there is a way out of the earthly text. They can, through the death of their bodies, escape the laws that govern and condition them, become authors themselves, experience their otherness. However, even in their afterlife of authorship there is a greater "Law," a greater structure that speaks them, which they cannot escape. Desire, like language, is always annulled, always put back, never actually grasped. Death as an object of desire, however, never really brings satisfaction, the appeasement of desire, but rather foregrounds the lack, the annulment of satisfaction. The desire for death, the "dead desire" is postponed and displaced.

This desire for death is a constant presence in Spark's work, a presence that works as the metonymy of the original desire for the construction of narratives. As Lacan suggests in "Function and Field of Speech and Language" "[T]he symbol manifests itself first of all as the murder of the thing, and this death constitutes in the subject the eternalization of his desire" (104). When the object of desire is reached, the truth of metonymy is revealed, and desire is once again canceled, in some cases transferred to another object. During this moment of revelation, the absence of *jouissance* is ever more present in the narratives.

NOTES

1. As Peter Brooks states in *Reading for the Plot*: "If we cannot do without plots, we nonetheless feel uneasy about them, and feel obliged to show up their arbitrariness, to parody their mechanisms while admitting our dependence on them" (7).

2. Her death as a teacher comes when she is expelled from school because Sandy accuses her of fascist inclinations: "Miss Brodie was forced to retire at the end of the summer, on the grounds that she had been teaching Fascism" (*PMJB* 125); her fictions are destroyed when it is Sandy instead of Rose who sleeps with Miss Brodie's beloved: "[I]n the event it was Sandy who slept with Teddy Lloyd and Rose who carried back the information" (*PMJB* 110); the death of her prime comes after the end of her teaching career.

3. The description of the painting in the novel is the following: "Job's wife, tall, sweet-faced, with the intimation of a beautiful body inside the large tent-like case of her firm clothes, bending, long-necked, solicitous over Job. In her hand is a lighted candle. It is night, it is winter; Job's wife wears a glorious red tunic over her dress. Job sits on a plain cube-shaped block. He might be in front of a fire, for the light of the candle alone cannot explain the amount of light that is cast on the two figures. Job is naked except for a loin-cloth. He clasps his hands above his knees. His body seems to shrink, but it is the shrunkness of pathos rather than want. Beside him is the piece of broken pottery that he has taken to scrape his wounds. His beard is thick. He is not an old man. Both are in their early prime, a couple in their thirties. (Indeed, their recently-dead children were not yet married.) His face looks up at his wife, sensitive, imploring some favour, urging some cause. What is his wife trying to tell him? What does he beg, this stricken man, so serene in his faith, so accomplished in argument?" (*OP* 76–77).

4. I put the word "self-inscription" in quotation marks, because, apart from the case of Frederick in *The Public Image*, the other deaths—mostly deaths of women—are rather complicated, in the sense that although the desire for the killing of the body is present, the actual act is never openly committed by the character. There is always the presence of another who undertakes the role of inscribing the body, as I will show later.

5. As Freud explains in *Beyond the Pleasure Principle*: "In the case of children's play we seemed to see that children repeat unpleasurable experiences for the additional reason that they can master a powerful impression far more thoroughly by being active than they could by merely experiencing it passively. Each fresh repetition seems to strengthen the mastery they are in search of. Nor can children have their *pleasurable* experience often enough, and they are inexorable in their insistence that the repetition shall be an identical one" (307).

6. Sibylla is a woman whom Apollo fell in love with and "sought to break [her] will with gifts"; she chose eternal life without asking for eternal youth. The god gave her eternal life "and promised endless youth as well, if [she] would yield to love." However, she remained "unwedded" and doomed to live eternally, until "time . . . will shrivel [her] . . . to but a tiny thing, and [her] limbs, consumed by age, will shrink to a feather's weight" (Ovid XIV, 130–148).

7. Pinewood is the material from which coffins are usually made.

8. From the beginning of her journey, Lise places special importance on the use of four languages—Danish, French, Italian, and English—and this follows her through to the end, when she orders her murderer to kill her "and repeats it in four languages" (*DS* 106); moreover, this emphasis is shared by the narrator who informs the reader that Lise's story and photograph will be "published in the newspapers of four languages."

9. The fact that Iowa is not in New Jersey further promotes the vanity of any quest for origins and realities in Lise's games with identities.

10. This sacrifice, with the stabs in the throat and the breast, could be read as an allusion to the sacrifice of women in Greek tragedy and myth. Especially the case of Polyxena, the daughter of Priamus, in the *Iliad*, which took place in order for the shadow of Achilles to be appeased, has a lot in common with the ritual of Lise's death. As Ovid describes it: "[W]hen she had been placed before the fatal altar and knew the grim rites were preparing for her; and when she saw Neoptolemus standing, sword in hand, with his eyes fixed upon her, she exclaimed: 'Spill at last my noble blood, for I am ready, and plunge your sword deep in my throat and breast!' (and she bared her throat and breast)" (Ovid XIII, 454–460).

11. Joan of Arc was associated with the cross throughout her lifetime, because she considered herself a crusader and the crucifix was a symbol of liberation for her, but more so at the moment of her death by burning, when "a Dominican consoled [her and she] asked him to hold high a crucifix for her to see and to shout out the assurances of salvation so loudly that she should hear him above the roar of the flames" (Lanhers 228).

12. Freud, in his work "Instincts and Their Vicissitudes," defines sadism as "the exercise of violence or power upon some other person as object," while masochism—"an expression of the feminine nature" (415)—as "the turning round of the sadistic instinct upon the subject's own self" (*On Metapsychology* 124).

13. It has been a long established myth of psychoanalysis that women are more narcissistic than men. According to Freud, "[W]ith the onset of puberty the maturing of the female sexual organs . . . seems to bring about an intensification of the original narcissism, and this is unfavourable of a true object-choice" (82).

14. This scene of interpenetration reminds one of the combat between Odysseus and the boar, which Robert Con Davis in his work *The Fictional Father* describes as follows: "Odysseus and the boar lock together in combat and pierce each other's bodies; and, for a moment, the two are united like lovers, their embrace breaking only as Odysseus' spear penetrates further and the beast dies. This scene is a highly concentrated tableau in which two figures first merge in a moment of unity that dis-solves subsequently when the spear cuts their bond and separates them with death . . . the movement of the spear and the tusk represents that phase of the Oedipal situation in which the father's law is asserted as a principle of opposition and difference" (20–21).

15. "According to the ancients, the panther is the only animal to emit a fragrant odour, which it uses to capture its victims. The panther has only to hide (his appearance strikes terror), and his victims are bewitched by his scent—an invisible trap to which they come to be caught" (Baudrillard, *Seduction* 76).

16. Aristotle, in his "Poetics," defines tragedy as "an imitation of an action . . . with incidents arousing pity and fear, whereby to provide an outlet for such emotions" (12).

4

Seduction of the Gaze: Spectacles and Images in *The Public Image*

[T]he heavenly fire no longer strikes depraved cities, it is rather the lens which cuts through ordinary reality like a laser, putting it to death.

—Jean Baudrillard
Simulations

What you seek is nowhere; but turn yourself away, and the object of your love will be no more. That which you behold is but the shadow of a reflected form and has no substance of its own. With you it comes, with you it stays, and it will go with you—if you can go.

—Ovid
Metamorphoses

Following the games with the *mises en abyme* of texts that seduce and kill with their power of inscription, Spark's later narratives focus on the same pattern, imposed this time by the so-called "outside." The world of the spectacle is foregrounded with special emphasis on the endless games one can play with images, which have come to replace the "real."

Appearances seem to manipulate even the word itself, to empty it of its meaning, to seduce meaning altogether. The power of appearances, mostly associated with the female in Spark's work, is used in order to play with traditional concepts of power, to undermine the reader's perception, to turn signs against themselves and finally seduce meaning into nonsense. Jean Baudrillard explains in *Seduction*: "All appearances conspire to combat and to root out meaning (whether intentional or otherwise), and turn it into a game, into another of the game's rules, a more arbitrary rule—or into another elusive ritual, one that is more adventurous and seductive than the directive line of meaning" (54).

In her novel *The Public Image*, Muriel Spark considers the theme of the double death that is entailed in the process of seeing: the death of the gaze and the death by the gaze. In her narrative the media kill the viewed by imprisoning them in the immobility of a representation and the viewers, as these representations do not belong to their eyes but are pre-shaped for them—thus celebrating the birth of the all-empowering spectacle of the image. Her world is dominated by simulation, "still and always the place of gigantic enterprise of manipulation, of control and of death" (Baudrillard, *Simulations* 182).

This new world of "blindness" completely negates the woman who becomes the Other, the image par excellence. As she has always been the receiver of the gaze, never the producer, the viewed, never the viewer, she is now the "negative" of representation. She cannot have power, since power belongs to those who control our vision and, through that, our representations. As Ann Kaplan comments in her work *Women and Film* "[The] positioning of the two sex genders in representation clearly privileges the male (through the mechanisms of voyeurism and fetishism, which are male operations, and because his desire carries power/action where woman's usually does not)" (29).

Willingly embracing her multiple selves, Annabel, the main character in the novel, delights in woman's close affinity with the "art" of lying. Annabel is a woman of multiple appearances, multiple masks, that she can put on or take off at will in order to gain her goals, thus leading the spectator/reader to the void of her fictions. It was Joan Riviere in her influential essay "Womanliness as a Masquerade" published in 1929, who introduced the concept of the female masquerade. Riviere points out that "Womanliness . . . could be assumed and worn as a mask, both to hide the possession of masculinity and to avert the reprisals expected if she was found to possess it" (33). However, the masculine "nature" of the woman is also presented as an artificial construct: "She has to treat the situation of displaying her masculinity to men as a 'game,' as something *not real*, as a 'joke'" (39, italics added). Illustrating how the interplay of conflicts in modern woman is resolved through the seduction of the masquerade, Riviere presents a void in the games with masks that women have to play, since both the feminine and masculine identity of her woman are treated as masks.

This void is celebrated in *The Public Image*, where the reader is presented with a continuous interplay of words, texts, voices, and spectacles associated with women. Origins are lost in a web of myths, stories, and histories, while the narrative becomes an endless *mise en abyme* of multiple texts that reflect the fictional process.

Muriel Spark plays with these images that ceaselessly interchange in her novel, thus enfolding her reader and characters in their power, leading, ultimately, to their utter annihilation. In almost all her novels and short stories, Muriel Spark forces us to inhabit the " Society of the Spectacle," as Guy Debord calls it, "where there is no new image under the sun—only images of images of images" (Kearney 171). Draining all relationships of emotions, she has her characters strive for an image that will render them invincible.

In *The Public Image*, the phenomenon of the hyperreal—"the phenomenon of an irradiating synthesis of combinatory models in a hyperspace without atmosphere" (Baudrillard, *Simulations* 3)—is even stronger than in Spark's other novels. Spectacle reigns and the world of the media has turned everything into a mere replica, a representation without an original image. Characters and public seem entangled in a spider's web that the media have spun around them. Spectacle is over and above everything, objects and people, the dead and the living. The central force in the novel is the woman's image, but the woman is nowhere to be found, as the lens has completely negated, annihilated her. In *Camera Lucida* Barthes observes: "[O]nce I feel myself observed by the lens, everything changes: I constitute myself in the process of 'posing,' I instantaneously make another body for myself, I transform myself in advance into an image. This transformation is an active one: I feel that the Photograph creates my body or mortifies it, according to its caprice" (10–11). So, in a paradoxical way it is the image that creates the body and not vice versa.

In the same way, the gods of the media create Annabel in their image, after their likeness, thus introducing her to the Edenic world of the spectacle she is to dominate. The process of Annabel's creation begins when she is discovered by an Italian director, Luigi Leopardi; however, she is actually created by Francesca, "a very small Italian woman of twenty-eight," whose "commission [was] to *build up* Annabel" (*PI* 23, italics added). The two gods, a male and a female that participate in the woman's creation, unite their forces to shape the (public) images of Annabel and her husband, Frederick.[1]

Annabel *is* the image, or rather images; her life as a character in the novel begins and ends with the image. Luigi Leopardi, the director, sees Annabel acting and she immediately becomes the Other of the film, the impression on the screen. The "thing" itself, the original "One" behind the replica, has disappeared and there is only the *reflection* in the mirror: "He [Luigi Leopardi] had noticed, *not Annabel*, but her recordable image, eyes that would change with the screen's texture, something sheerly given in the face, like a gift that could be exercised— he had seen this at first and second glance" (*PI* 93, italics added). She is like the negative of a film, the "*not*-Annabel," which makes us wonder, who is *the* Annabel and in what way is she different from her recordable image?

Significantly, it is the eyes that first seduce the gaze, and are seduced by the gaze. It is only through the "silent, immobile orgasm" (Baudrillard, *Seduction* 77) of the contact of eyes that seduction reigns. In this case it is not a simple process of two gazes that are caught in an erotic duel but of multiple gazes that catch and kill one another in their own discourse. It is Annabel's eyes that capture Luigi's; it is Luigi's perception that imprisons Annabel's eyes within his discourse; and it is finally the lens of the camera, the eye of the public that is seduced by the tiger's eyes and seduces the public with its power.

It is, in other words, a double process of killing and getting killed through the image. The gaze of the Medusa turns others into stone, but it is also turned into stone itself by looking at its own reflection, its deadly gaze.[2] It is through the gaze that this process of construction imposes itself on Annabel, turning her into the Other of the screen; it is Annabel's eyes that portray her "tigerness," and it is these eyes that primarily seduce the gaze. It is "only" through her eyes, the organ of sight, that the spectacle is primarily created; Annabel sees through her eyes, and she is seen, perceived through her eyes. It is remarkable how much sight can deceive the viewed and the viewers, since what they see is not what is, but a mere construction: "The simulacrum is never that which conceals the truth—it is the truth which conceals that there is none. The simulacrum is true" (Baudrillard, *Selected Writings* 166). Annabel's eyes become a mirror where the images of others are reflected. And the eyes, the gaze of the others, become a mirror for her vision where she sees the reflection of herself as the Lady-Tiger. She becomes the Lady-Tiger that the others see in her, the tamed temptress that the popular mythology wants her to be. What does she see when she looks but an image of herself which others have naturalized and she has internalized?

This is the function that is found at the heart of the institution of the subject in the visible. What determines me, at the most profound level, in the visible, is the gaze that is outside. It is through the gaze that I enter light and it is from the gaze that I receive its effects. Hence it comes about that the gaze is the instrument through which light is embodied and through which . . . I am *photo-graphed*. (Lacan, "Of the Gaze as *Objet Petit a*" 106)

Annabel is "photo-graphed" through the lens; the spotlight that falls on her has the power to transform her from the "little slip of a thing" that she used to be into the English Lady-Tiger: "Annabel was still a little slip of a thing, but her face had changed, as if by action of many famous cameras, into a mould of her public figuration. She looked aloof and well bred. Her smile had formerly been quick and small, but now it was slow and somewhat formal; nowadays she was vivacious only when the time came, in front of the cameras, to play the tiger" (*PI* 35). She has become a "mould of her public figuration" that can give hundreds of reproductions. But this mold is not produced from an original: it "originates" from an image. It is the figuration of a figuration, the image of another image. This is a parody of the world of postmodernism where, according to Derrida, "there is no longer an original light, deriving from the God-Sun of Platonism or from the imagination-lamp of humanism. There is only a circling of reflections without beginning or end—the 'mirror of a mirror . . . a reference without a referent, without any first or last unit, a ghost that is the phantom of no flesh, wandering about without a past, without any death, birth or present'" (as quoted in Kearney, 177).

In *The Public Image*, the reader is introduced into this game with images that destroys all "originals." The myth of the Medusa's gaze is transformed into another game that leads to a series of murders by the gaze. Annabel looks at the camera and the camera returns her look, transformed and imprisoning, turning her into stone, a Medusa gaze that is reflected in the mirror and kills the Medusa into a stone image, the horrible reflection of a radical otherness that captures both the others' gaze but also its own eyes into its seduction. Jean-Pierre Vernant in his work *Mortals and Immortals* captures this game with the Gorgo's gaze: "The face of the Gorgo is the Other, your double. . . . It is a simple reflection and yet also a reality from the world beyond, an image that captures you because instead of merely returning to you the appearance of your own face and refracting your gaze, it represents in its grimace the terrifying horror of a radical otherness with which you yourself will be identified as you are turned to stone" (138). Annabel creates the mask, the Other, which returns her gaze and kills her. In her case it is a series of masks and a series of murders that kill not only Annabel, but also everyone who is seduced into looking at the image.

Annabel's first death comes with the image of the English Lady-Tiger, the identification of the woman and the tiger, another instance of woman's equation with nature and the values of the natural.[3] Through the eyes of the camera the woman becomes an exotic and remote object, offered for consumption. Man is excited by this animality of the woman; he is excited and at the same time afraid. She is the wild tiger in the screen/cage and he, the tamer with the camera/whip, has her under his control. But the fear that she may get loose and devour him is always lurking in his mind, the devouring tiger perhaps associated with the devouring vagina that will envelop man and capture him in her dark "unknown." "Men have never tired of fashioning expressions for the violent force by which man feels himself drawn to the woman, and side by side with his longing, the dread that through her he might die and be undone" (Kaplan 31).

It seems that Luigi Leopardi, and all men through him, looks and sees the object of his desire: the tiger of his dreams, the tiger that will satisfy his sexual drives, that will match his "leopard-like" nature—another instance of the analogy of Eros and Thanatos, desire and death. The moment he has found the animal that he was looking for, his male gaze behind the camera kills the woman into a representation, creating "the day-dream of the wild animal-woman, the sexual beast, an image which is becoming even more pressing today after a long suppression of desire" (Kappeler 75). Annabel represents the beautiful, wild tiger—its roars so sexually arousing—the female that man has always wanted to master and tame.

Through the power of the lens Annabel becomes "a twentieth century Jane Eyre", "She is certainly a 'tiger in the tank'", "The scene in the garden where she glides into the children's secret lair with an expression of terrifying serenity . . . the effect of external propriety with a tiger in her soul . . . something between Jane Eyre, a heroine of D. H. Lawrence, and the governess in *The Turn of the Screw*. . . ." (*PI* 20). In this hyperreal world , this world of simulations it is only the image, the Other that exists, and who could be a better Other than the woman who has always been assigned this role to play. The reporters tell the public that "*she* is" the tiger, *she* is the image. The process of her construction, according to Luigi, is so powerful that it has turned Annabel into a likeness of her image. Like another creator, he expects her to become the image now, since she is in his possession: "It's what I began to make of you that you've partly become" (*PI* 34).

However, the novel seems to be playing with the idea of the dominance of the active male gaze and the passivity of the female behind the camera. Annabel participates in the mythologies that are formed around her by her own free will. As the narrator informs us "Annabel . . . was entirely aware of the image-making process in every phase" (*PI* 27); man, in this case, is associated with the passive victim of the lens, the one who lacks knowledge, who cannot achieve action: "Frederick hardly knew what was going on" (*PI* 25) until he suddenly "[finds] himself rooted deeply and with serious interest in a living part" (*PI* 27). He is not only in the shadow of the woman's charm, he is also in the shadow of her intelligence; he may have the power to kill her with his gaze, but she has the power of knowledge. After all, it was she who first ate from the forbidden fruit of representation.

She seems to know that she is totally immersed in representation. The medium is everywhere always; even when it is absent, its presence is in the air, lurking above our heads; there is a vague feeling that the all-seeing eye of the camera is following us, replacing the all-seeing eye of God, immobilizing us in space and time, imprisoning us in the image. We are led by this eye, our gaze dead as we peep into Annabel's private/public life. Both Annabel and Frederick are caught in their "living parts," an oxymoron used to reveal how the sudden and thorough invasion of the media into their lives has made them unable to distinguish between life and role, acting and being; for them the part *is* their life. Thus Billy, Frederick's closest friend, accuses Annabel of posing when she thinks she is just being "herself": "'Oh, stop posing,' Billy said. She was standing on the carpet, one hand on a side-table, gazing back into her youth, as if playing a middle-aged part. 'I'm not posing,' she said, and flopped into a chair" (*PI* 14). Annabel's life is a constant performance, grasped as she is by the power of images, since as Lacan states: "To imitate is no doubt to reproduce an image. But at bottom, it is, for the subject, to be inserted in a function whose exercise grasps it" ("Of the Gaze as *Object Petit a*" 100).

But it isn't only Annabel and Frederick that are grasped by the image. The eye of the camera perceives, is perceived, seduces and is seduced, kills with its power. It becomes once again the deadly gaze of the Gorgon, which represents the Power of death, as Jean-Pierre Vernant explains:

To see the Gorgon is to look her in the eyes and, in the exchange of gazes, to cease to be oneself, a living being, and to become, like her, a Power of death. To stare at Gorgon is to lose one's sight in her eyes and to be transformed into stone, an unseeing, opaque object. . . . Fascination means that man can no longer detach his gaze and turn his face away from this Power; it means that his eye is lost in the eye of this Power, which looks at him as he looks at it, and that he himself is thrust into the world over which this Power resides. (137)

The public is lured into this deadly "Power" of the tiger's gaze and is lost in the Edenic world of the image. It is imprisoned by the camera, in the perception of these naturalized myths, so that the receivers of all these significations are unaware of the whole process of mythmaking and unable to react to it. They too become an inextricable part of the process of mythmaking, inserted into imitation, grasped by it:

[I]n the event, Frederick found himself rooted deeply and with serious interest in a living part such as many multitudes believe exists: a cultured man without temperament, studious, sportsmanlike, aristocratic, and a fatherly son of Mother Earth, Annabel's husband. As for Annabel, she was portrayed cool and equal to him in all respects, except that she was a tiger-woman at heart and in "the secret part of their lives." This tiger was portrayed only by her eyes; it was an essential part of the public image that the tiger quality was always restrained in public. (*PI* 27)

Actually it is not what the public sees, but what it is allowed to see, that makes the difference. They only have access to the result of the process and not to the process itself. That is why the "multitudes" believe that there is something behind the image. Lacan writes about the imperative for the human psyche to believe in the reality of "things": "[W]hen I am presented with a representation, I assure myself that I know quite a lot about it, I assure myself as a consciousness that knows that it is only representation, and that there is, beyond, the thing, the thing itself" ("Of the Gaze as *Objet petit a*" 106). It is this belief that causes the public to be so deceived. Even those who can see deeper into the lie and understand what is going on, even they cannot react but only accept this as a natural part of their lives: "[T]he more sophisticated readers simply repeated the Italian proverb 'If it isn't true, it's to the point'" (*PI* 28).

The public's gaze is captured within the lens, unable to control what it sees or how it sees. Isn't this the ultimate murder of the gaze? Are they the possessors of their eyes or are they just eyes that gaze and cannot see anything but what has been set before them? The object that they look at was pre-shaped in their minds, so they cannot escape it. The image precedes the gaze— "precession of simulacra"—like the map that "precedes" and "engenders" the territory (Baudrillard, *Simulations* 166).

However, as I explained above, this whole process of the seductive gaze is turned into a game by the author, who touches upon the hilarious nature of seeing and believing through the media. In the case of Annabel and Frederick Christopher:

It was somehow felt that the typical Englishman, such as Frederick Christopher was, had always really concealed a foundry of smouldering sex beneath all that expressionless reserve. It was suggested in all the articles that cited the Christopher image, that this was a fact long known to the English themselves, but only now articulated. Later, even some English came to believe it, and certain English wives began to romp in bed far beyond the call of their husbands, or the capacities of their years, or any of the realities of the situation. (*PI* 28)

The public, the receivers of the mythologies about Annabel get caught in this game of simulations the media offer them. Their lives become part of an electronic game, where anybody can live any kind of experience through a simulation model. According to Freud, active scopophilia—"taking others as objects, subjecting them to a controlling and curious gaze" (Mulvey 8)—is "one of the component instincts of sexuality" (Mulvey 8). In the exploitation of this instinct and through the production of images that are looked at, cinema offers the public what Laura Mulvey calls "sexual satisfaction through sight" (10), through "identification with the image seen"(10). In other words, when people look at the screen "curiosity and the wish to look intermingle with a fascination with likeness and recognition" (9). Women identify with the image of the English Lady-Tiger that they watch in the magic screen, and men have the fascination of looking at the object of their desire, taking the position of the consuming/devouring male gaze. The lens of the camera has offered them the screen through which they perceive their simulation model—Annabel and her husband—that satisfies their need for a more "exotic" sexual life.

Publicity turns both Annabel and Frederick into objects that are looked at, part of a spectacle that will satisfy the deeper instincts of the viewers. Apart from being the English Lady-Tiger, Annabel must in addition experience her second death through the image of the perfect wife: "They [Annabel and Frederick] always patched up their rows, went out together, were accustomed to each other. Moreover, they were proud of each other in the eyes of their expanding world where he was considered to be deeply interesting and she highly talented" (*PI* 17–18).

Annabel and Frederick are further fragmented in the "photo-graphs" that Francesca arranges for them, displaying the "perfect couple" to a public who experience their *jouissance* through the media images. According to Barthes: "'[M]yself' never coincides with my image; for it is the image which is heavy, motionless, stubborn (which is why society sustains it), and 'myself' which is light, divided, dispersed" (*Camera Lucida* 12). Through these photographs the image becomes the all-powerful force in the narrative; Annabel and Frederick's bodies become the "Spectrum"[4] of the photograph, first mortified and then re-created by the power of the lens to murder and, at the same time, give life:

Francesca would come, either to talk to them, or to arrange an interview, or with a photographer to take a picture of Annabel lounging on the bed, in her night-dress, one shoulder-band slipping down her arm and her hair falling over part of her face. Francesca disarranged the bed. Frederick on the edge of the bed, in a Liberty dressing-gown, smoking, with a smile as of recent reminiscence. Or else Francesca had them photographed with a low table set with a lace-edged tray of afternoon tea, and the sun streaming in the window. Frederick held his cup and seemed to be stirring it gently and gravely while Annabel, sweet but unsmiling, touched the silver teapot with a gracious hand. (*PI* 26)

The detailed signs here construct the composite image. The arrangement of the scene clarifies the implication that they have just finished making wild love (Annabel with disarranged hair, shoulder-band slipping down her arm, Frederick smoking with a smile of recent reminiscence). The "hidden camera" creates "through artificial composition and posing" the impression of "a peep through the key-hole" (Kappeler 73–74). This "hidden" part of their lives is revealed through the visual image, which is much more powerful than language, since it can hide and at the same time reveal, give and at the same time withhold information, strip and at the same time dress, exposing the unexposable. Without being provocative, which would have insulted the very offendable Italian public, it manages to represent a covert display of potentially pornographic dimensions. As Barthes suggests about the nature of the spectacle, the viewers are no longer interested "whether the passion is genuine or not. What the public wants is the image of passion, not passion itself. ... what is expected is the intelligible representation of moral situations which are usually private. This emptying out of interiority to the benefit of its exterior signs, this exhaustion of the content by the form, is the very principle of triumphant classical art" (*Mythologies* 18).

The other arrangement with the couple drinking their tea will offer the right balance for those whose imagination would lead them to different routes of thought than those expected by the arranger; the tea-drinking moment with Frederick's paternal image gently and gravely stirring the liquid and Annabel unsmilingly touching the teapot, assign the right degree of gravity and seriousness to the two characters to temper its risqué possibilities. Importance is placed on the quality of the objects in the photograph, the *lace-edged* tray and the *silver* teapot—lace being a token of the English tradition and silver being a sign of gentility. Objects and characters mix so well that the one finally seems to blend into the other.

Of course, in both these representative photographs of the couple's private life the woman plays the role of the (consumable) object.[5] Again the audience is interested in the fictional image of the couple, where the woman must serve the man/father. That's why Annabel is still in bed, while Frederick is already sitting smoking a cigarette, presumably in control of the situation. After he has satisfied her he can take a rest. He must be away from her since a position near her would naturally diminish his masculinity. In the tea-drinking moment, he is already drinking his tea, when Annabel is touching the teapot, probably in order to serve herself after serving him first. According to Clare Brant, "[T]hrough the elaborations of tea ceremonies men kept women serviceable . . . and further imposed a heterosexual erotics on the activity, reinforced by metaphors which link the fragility of china to women and their reputations" (249).

However, despite all the above significations, Annabel is the major presence in the novel and dominates the scene. Without her, Frederick is nothing, he does not exist. We are confronted with a reversal in the sexual order of creation; the original Christian myth has God creating man before woman, naming her after him. In the novel not only is Frederick, the man, created from the shadow of the woman and in the likeness of her image, but she is also the dominant force in their relationship, reducing him to the role of the servant in her story. He is not just a paternal figure that the bedroom photograph presents; he is also the "fatherly son of Mother Earth, Annabel's husband" that the narrator wrote him to be. He is "fatherly" only in the photographs; elsewhere he is a "son" of Mother Earth. Annabel is, by implication, assigned the title of Mother Earth, another allusion to the construct of the all-encompassing force that she stands for in the novel.

Frederick, therefore, resorts to a spectacular suicide in order to master the structures that imprison him in a role of passivity he cannot tolerate. His death will be the major plot in the world of the cinema that is controlled by "plots." Frederick wants to disrupt the "rarefaction . . . of the speaking subjects" whereby "none shall enter the order of discourse if he does not satisfy certain requirements or if he is not, from the outset, qualified to do so", as Foucault suggests ("The Order of Discourse" 61–62). The spectacle of his suicide grants him entrance into the order of discourse, which he can now manipulate with his absence.

Frederick, a professional plotter since he is a scriptwriter, attempts to create the controlling plot and destroy the plots that were suffocating him. According to Whittaker: "Frederick . . . begins to apply the techniques of fiction to real life. Having lived in a world of scenarios and watched the re-creation of his wife by professionals, Frederick has learned about plots—their design, execution and reverberations. He formulates a real-life plot to rival that created by the film industry, designed to smash Annabel's career" (113). What Ruth Whittaker fails to observe in her comments is that there is no "real life" in the novella. What the reader receives is merely a hyperreality, a vicious circle of simulacra.

The husband is, during the first stage, the power that speaks the woman,[6] but as the novel proceeds and the woman moves toward the powerful stage of the temptress, he loses his power. For the public his death, which comes approximately in the middle of the novel, means that he is the victim of the temptress. But for the reader, through his death he is apparently trying to regain the power he has lost. It seems that in all Muriel Spark's novels at the moment the woman starts to gain power the man gradually deteriorates and loses his strength. Thus, in a last effort to regain control the husband resorts to a reproduction of the most powerful image of death, to destroy all other representations.

Annabel's husband dies a spectacular death of his choice—jumping from a church of the martyrs of St. John and St. Paul to the catacombs below: "He jumped from there to the foundations where they have placed the martyrdom of St Paul" (*PI* 56). This spectacular suicide is an overflow of images that drains death of its content, conveying other, more important significations. Until now, others spoke for Frederick, but now, with his death, he speaks for himself for the first time; nobody can die for him, death is the only action that he can do for himself, where he can be the only leading actor, creating for himself the major script.

Frederick had threatened Annabel that he would commit suicide by jumping out of a window in order to destroy her public image, a very poor death indeed for the perfectionist that Frederick was. After a visit to the Church of St. John and St. Paul with Annabel, he realizes that the site, so full of signs and memories, is the ideal place for his last act. Annabel, recalling this visit, gives the following account:

They had stood on the edge of the staircase that had been built for visitors to the church. It had made her dizzy to see so many levels of winding passageways, layer upon layer. Later, they had gone down by the stairs, part of the way, and traversed some of the excavated planes of the old houses and pagan temples that lay ruggedly within the intestines of the excavation. There, by tradition, was the house where two Roman officers had lived, converts to Christianity. This was the place of their martyrdom. Carved stone plaques in the wall had pointed the way. "In these catacombs, these passages, their blood was spilt." "Here, they were brought. . . ." (*PI* 57)

The diction Annabel uses when reliving this past experience bestows on it a more complex set of symbols, so that it transcends a simple visit to a church. It seems that for her the trip was not to the catacombs but to the center of the earth, the "intestines" of the body, perhaps that of Mother Earth that bore the two Romans who spilled their blood for Christianity.

It is this symbolism Frederick wants to exploit to the full in order to associate himself with sainthood and to turn Annabel into the devil-woman who bewitches and destroys men. However, again Frederick is an absent presence in this visit; we can only marvel at the thoughts that led him to the choice of this particular death at this place. Could it be that he wanted his death to be read as a visit to the intestines of the body, a union with his body—so alienated from him through the process of Annabel's image making—or the body of the Catholic Church?[7] This cinematographic action is immediately perceived by Annabel as a script that Frederick the scriptwriter leaves behind him in order to destroy Annabel's public image, in other words Annabel herself, since she *is* the image. She seems to be caught up in her husband's text.

Through his death Frederick can produce his text, as is evident by the letters he leaves behind to be read after he is dead, or his "suicide notes" addressed to his dead mother, to Annabel, to his newborn son, and to his lover. It is only after his absence—and through this absence—from the narrative that he can make his presence felt, that his text can be read and made dominant in the novella. Through his death Frederick re-creates some popular myths of our culture, which imprison the woman in certain roles. In his letter to his mother he explains what has led him to his death: "Orgies—outrageous orgies of the most licentious nature are given in her honour, far into the night. Sometimes I have gone to persuade her to come home from these scenes of evil, and horror, but she laughs at me and induces her friends to laugh also" (*PI* 85). He places Annabel in an environment of black magic, evil and horror where she seems to be the high priestess, in whose honor the orgies are given. In the eyes of the public she is now the temptress, the evil force that has led her husband to his "fall," a form of female death figure. So, now she must "fall" with him; she must be expelled from the Edenic world of the media.

With his letter to his "true" and "wonderful" mother he seeks to dethrone Annabel from the pious image of Madonna/Mother Earth, alluding to the popular division of mother/whore: "I thank you Mamma, for the wonderful things you have done for me. Pray for me. Would that all women were like you" (*PI* 84). This is a letter to the Mother, to the Mother of all men, to the all-encompassing Italian "Mamma," that Annabel can never be.

The divine, innocent Madonna becomes, all of a sudden, a new Eve, the female temptress, the real, evil Lady-Tiger that lures man to his destruction. Suddenly, we get caught in the plot of James's *The Turn of the Screw*,[8] a plot that, according to Blanchot follows this blueprint:

the ambiguity of innocence, of an innocence which is pure of the evil it contains; the art of perfect dissimulation which enables the children to conceal this evil from the honest folk amongst whom they live, an evil which is perhaps an innocence that becomes evil in the proximity of such folk, the incorruptible innocence they oppose to the true evil of adults; or again the riddle of the visions attributed to them, the uncertainty of a story which has perhaps been foisted upon them by the demented imagination of a governess who tortures them to death with her own hallucinations. (*The Sirens' Song* 81)

This seems like another comment of the author on the power of simulation in the spectacle and the ambiguous nature of images and mythologies. What is Annabel after all? Who is she and what are her characteristics? Is she truly the innocent creature she poses to be, whom others accuse of being evil, and "torture [her] to [the] death [of her image] with [their] own hallucinations"? Is she an evil presence who hides her true nature behind the image of innocence? Where is the truth and where is the lie? The press, the public want to know. But, as Blanchot very rightly puts it in his comment on *The Turn of the Screw* "the pressure the governess exerts on the children to extract their secret from them, which the supernatural too, doubtless, exerts upon them, . . . primarily is the pressure of narration itself, the wonderful, terrible pressure exerted on reality by the act of writing—that anguish, torture, violence, finally conducive to death where everything seems to be revealed, yet everything reverts to uncertainty, void and darkness" (*The Sirens' Song* 85).

This "void and darkness" dominates the novella from now on. All "certainties" evaporate and leave the reader/spectator in a void of inexplicable and controversial signs. For the reader, it seems that Frederick is the devil, the poisonous snake who, through the reproduction of the image of death, drags Annabel outside Eden into hell; a hell that is very clearly perceived by Annabel in a moment of illumination, during a trance, after she has recognized Frederick's body in the hospital:

[She] was driven home through the intertwining dark-lit streets, under the high-flying white flags of washing that swayed from window to window of the old palaces. The poisoner behind the black window-square, a man flattened against a wall with the daggers ready . . . she wondered how the film would end, and although she wanted to leave the cinema and go home, she wanted first to see the end. They drove round a deserted piazza with a fountain playing heartlessly, its bowl upheld by a group of young boys, which was built by the political assassin to placate his conscience; and past the palace of the cardinal who bore the sealed quiet of the whole within his guilt; with that girl now binding his body with her long hair for fun; while he lay planning, with a cold mind, the actions of the morning which were to conceal the night's evil: calumny, calumny, a messenger here and there, many messengers, bearing whispers and hints, and assured, plausible, eye-witness accusations; narrow streets within narrower; along beside the fearful walls of the Cenci palace, in one of the lanes where she had run from the party, looking for a taxi. The camera swung round to the old ghetto. Fixed inventions of deeds not done, accusations, the determined blackening of character. The doctor at her side said, "There are the news-people at your door, but I shall order them back. Stay in the car, and I'll park round the corner."

She said, "Wait a minute, I want to see it through to the end." (*PI* 60)

Frederick managed to drag her into the dark labyrinth of his script, so well portrayed by the "inter-twining dark-lit streets" that become narrower and narrower, leading to "the end." He is the "poisoner . . . with the daggers ready" to strike. Nightmare personified, Frederick is there to kill the image and leave Annabel an empty simulacrum. And Annabel can clearly recognize the film quality of her life. It is made explicit that her "reality" is now immersed in the film industry, a film itself, where she has taken the double role of leading actress and spectator who "want[s] to see it through to the end."

From this moment onward, we experience a significant transformation in the novel: the woman is totally immersed in simulation, becoming lost in the darkness of the brightly lit sites with the cameras, where she continuously kills herself in representations, not the passive product of the images' construction any more but the active producer of these images. However, although Frederick may have been seeking to enhance his image through his death, the paradoxical outcome is a further enhancement of Annabel's image. As Ruth Whittaker suggests: "For all her warmth as a mother, Annabel is none the less a very Sparkian woman; using all her skill as an actress and a creator of fictions, she briskly and efficiently reorganises events in her favour" (113). The characters have set out on a game of power, where the winner is the commander of the gaze. Annabel wants to undertake this role too, so she now becomes the producer of the image, construct and constructor at the same time. Hers is the male gaze, she is the generator of power, the force that kills herself in representation, as we can see in the following arrangement of the scene for the reporters:

Annabel sat on the chair left vacant for her. The neighbours with their instinct for ceremony and spectacle, had arranged those chairs which they had brought from their own best rooms in two semi-circles which flanked the best chair of all; this was upholstered in red velvet, and its arms were antiquely carved. With equal instinct, Annabel sat on this best chair and adjusted the baby. The press would soon arrive. The men sat modestly regarding the floor with their hands on their knees, they had taken advantage of the furniture-fetching to brush their hair and shoes and to put on a respectable necktie or at least a white shirt. (*PI* 67)

Annabel produces one of the most imposing images of life in Christianity—Madonna and Child—to attack the image of death. Italian society, the host of Roman Catholicism, is the perfect context for this image, as the Madonna as the very epitome of beauty and grace is more revered in Catholicism than in all other Christian religions. Annabel has become the image of motherhood par excellence, beginning with the ancient construct of Mother Earth and finishing with the contemporary construct of the Madonna.

The narrator later informs us that "the worthy scene, arranged as it was with Annabel and infant in its midst, [was] like some portrayal of a family and household by Holbein" (*PI* 72). To offer one more version of the picture, it would be appropriate to mention here that this reference to Holbein may have been to his famous painting "The Virgin with the family of Burgomaster Meyer" described by Freud in one of his letters to his fiancée after a visit to the Dresden museum. "Several ugly women and graceless young Miss kneel in front of the Madonna on the right, on the left a man with a monkish face holds a boy. The Madonna holds a boy in her arms and looks with such holy expression down to the praying people" (as quoted in Gombrich's "Freud's Aesthetics," 221). In the particular painting the narrator is probably referring to, the Madonna is very persuasive. According to Freud "Holbein's [Madonna] is neither woman nor girl, her sublimity and holy humility excludes any further questioning" (as quoted in Gombrich, 223).

This is the image Annabel wants to present to the public through the media. "[H]er sublimity and holy humility excludes any further questioning"; the journalists have no choice but to follow her "spontaneous" arrangement, their gaze imprisoned in hers:

[The press] found Annabel suitably arranged, with her neighbours now suddenly silent, sitting and standing around her with folded hands, hands open as if in appeal for pity, hands crossed on breasts, hands at throat in the gesture of sudden disaster, hands in despair, holding the side of the head, and in every other spontaneous attitude of feeling by which they could convey to the newcomers their sense of plight and solidarity with the bereft woman, just as successfully as if the scene had been studied and rehearsed for weeks. It would have been very nearly impossible, and certainly very hazardous, for any member of the press to ask Annabel an awkward or hostile question at the gathering, or to probe very far into the delicacy of the hour. Annabel blinked her eyes' moisture, swallowed visibly, looked down at the baby and sighed. (*PI* 68–69)

The woman is humble and divine, but for the reader it is the presence of the neighbors that gives gravity to the image, their hands acting as sole bearers of meaning, threatening the reporters. It is only the hands and not the faces that the reader is allowed to perceive, the narrator acting as his/her eyes, controller of the gaze, drawing a different picture, thus disrupting the image of Holbein's painting that was offered to Annabel's public a minute ago. The narrator, as very often happens in Spark's work, builds up an image for the sole purpose of shattering it later in order to make this destructive process ever more impressive.

To return to Holbein's painting, despite the "humility and sublimity" of the Madonna, it clearly alludes to the shallowness and emptiness of which Frederick accused Annabel. Holbein's painting is a product of the sixteenth century, a period of immense crisis in art when "[the general belief was that] nothing remained to be done because everything art could possibly do had been achieved" (Gombrich, *The Story of Art* 277). Art could be nothing but a replica of other works of art, an image of the image. Holbein was a master of the art of imitation and this painting of the Madonna is, according to Gombrich, "one of the most perfect examples of its kind . . . remind[ing] us of the most harmonious compositions of the Italian Renaissance, of Giovanni Bellini and Raphael" (*The Story of Art* 288–289).

This painting also offers us an allusion to the iconological crisis in religion, as it was painted during the period when there was a lot of controversy over the issue of the use of icons in the church. The way the whole process of the production of the image of Madonna-child-neighbors is manipulated by Annabel and presented to the reader, ridiculing the divinity of the Holy Mother and the Christ Child, justifies, I believe, the iconoclasts' anxiety about the death of the divine, because "the images concealed nothing at all, and . . . in fact they were not images, such as the original model would have made them, but actually perfect simulacra forever radiant with their own fascination" (Baudrillard, *Simulations* 9).

Holbein's "Virgin, whose calm and majestic figure is framed by a niche of classical forms," where the dominant form is a huge open shell, offers another allusion to a metaphor that is used by Frederick in the novel, the comparison between Annabel, the woman, and an empty shell. As he accuses her in a posthumous letter addressed to her: "You are a beautiful shell, like something washed up on the sea-shore, a collector's item, perfectly formed, a pearly shell—but empty, devoid of the life it once held" (*PI* 92). Bachelard informs us that "[T]he shell, for the Ancients, was the symbol of the human being in its entirety, body and soul. . . . Thus, they said, the body becomes lifeless when the soul has left it, in the same way that the shell becomes incapable of moving when it is separated from the part that give it life" (*The Poetics of Space* 116).

It is this emptiness that, according to Frederick, has led him to his suicide. The shell has become for him a trap that has lured him into it and devoured him.[9] It seems that "the true function of the organ of the eye, the eye filled with voracity, the evil eye" (115), as Lacan calls it, has fallen on Annabel and destroyed her. She had been under the gaze of others for so long that their evil eye has caused her to be expelled from Eden.

So, we come to the exodus, when Annabel takes her baby and is lost among the crowd at the airport leaving the world of the media behind her, on her way to Greece. Although she is not wearing her "dark glasses," she is not recognized. It seems that her fall from the Lady-Tiger image and her entrance into another has completely altered her appearance:[10]

Waiting for the order to board, she felt both free and unfree. The heavy weight of the bags was gone; she felt as if she was still, curiously, pregnant with the baby, but not pregnant in fact. She was pale as a shell. She did not wear her dark glasses. Nobody recognized her as she stood, having moved the baby to rest on her hips, conscious also of the baby in a sense weightlessly and perpetually within her, as an empty shell contains, by its very structure, the echo and harking image of former and former seas. (*PI* 124–125)

The metaphor of the shell prevails in this imagery. According to the narrator, she is a shell and an empty one but with a different emptiness from the one Frederick accused her of having, since even an empty shell "contains, by its very structure, the echo and harking image of former and former seas." The narrator here seems to adopt Robinet's view that "'fossils are alive . . . if not from the standpoint of an exterior form of life, for the reason that they lack perhaps certain limbs and senses . . . at least from that of an interior, hidden form of life, which is very real of its kind'" (as quoted in Bachelard's *The Poetics of Space*, 113).[11]

Like the ideal American wife of the TV-verite experiment that Baudrillard comments on, Annabel, another ideal heroine "[was] chosen, as in sacrificial rites, to be glorified and to die under the fiery glare of the studio lights, a modern fatum. For the heavenly fire no longer strikes depraved cities, it is rather the lens which cuts through ordinary reality like a laser, putting it to death" (*Simulations* 51). Annabel has experienced this death from the lens, her murder from her image. However, now it seems that it is her turn to kill the image and gain life from its death. The image's life has proved her death, and vice versa. The narrator tells us that she is not a completely empty shell, she *contains* "the echo and harking image of former and former seas"; however, what she contains is nothing but an image, a mere construct, as if she is unable to escape her conditioning. She is both free and unfree, pregnant and not pregnant, present but also absent, alive and dead.

So, could we say that Annabel managed to escape? Or is it just another world of images that she is entering? Instead of restoring the reader to the "real" as would be expected after the trip into the world of simulation, the narrator returns us again to the imaginary, the inside, the place of no return. It seems that there is no escaping this world of darkness and absence. There is a promise of an echo filling the gap, but the uncertainty remains. Perhaps there is no way out of the world of images or shadows. It is very difficult to escape from this world of the shadows, once you have entered it; to go back to my epigraph in this chapter, I believe it is important at this stage to quote the words of Ovid: "What you seek is nowhere; but turn yourself away, and the object of your love will be no more. That which you behold is but the shadow of a reflected form and has no substance of its own. With you it comes, with you it stays, and it will go with you—if you can go" (155). The myth has it that Narcissus never managed to escape the fascination of the image: "And even when he had been received into the infernal abodes, he kept on gazing on his image in the Stygian pool" (Ovid 159).[12]

The woman, although seemingly distant from the masquerade, cannot totally separate herself from appearances. The ambiguous ending undermines her ultimate liberation from the seduction of the spectacle.

NOTES

1. According to the Gnostic interpretation of the Bible, of which Peggy Reeves Sanday informs us in her book *Female Power and Male Dominance*: "[S]everal Gnostic theologians concluded from their interpretation of Genesis 1:26–7 that God is dyadic ('Let *us* make humanity') and that 'humanity which was formed according to the image and likeness of God (Father and Mother) was masculo-feminine'" (227).

2. According to the myth, the Medusa was a repulsive Monster with snakes for hair, that killed men by turning them to stone when they looked at her. However, Perseus manages to kill her with the help of Athena who gives him a shiny shield and tells him not to look at the Medusa's face. Perseus beheads Medusa and gives her head to Athena who puts it on her shield.

3. Bram Dijkstra in the *Idols of Perversity* informs us about "Carl Vogt's observation that 'whenever we perceive an approach to the animal type, the female is nearer to it than the male,' and that in any such male/female comparison 'we should discover a greater resemblance if we were to take the female as our standard'" (290).

4. As Barthes explains: "[T]he person or thing photographed is the target, the referent, a kind of little simulacrum, any *eidolon* emitted by the object, which I should like to call the *Spectrum* of the Photograph, because this word retains, through its root, a relation to 'spectacle' and adds to it that rather terrible thing which is there in every photograph: the return of the dead" (*Camera Lucida* 9).

5. Although there is a woman behind the camera, her gaze is the male-oriented gaze of popular culture. As Ann Kaplan points out: "The gaze is not necessarily male (literally), but to own and activate the gaze, given our language and the structure of the unconscious, is to be in the 'masculine' position" (30).

6. In the beginning of the novel we learn that "her husband, when she was in the company of his friends . . . tolerantly and quite affectionately insinuated the fact of her stupidity, and she accepted this without resentment for as long as it did not convey to her any sense of contempt" (*PI* 9). There are also many other instances of Frederick insinuating similar "facts" and Annabel accepting them as God-given.

7. There is a glimpse of what Frederick intended to achieve through the choice of that particular place for the execution of his suicide in his posthumous letter to his dead mother: "Unworthy, I die with the Holy Martyrs in the hope of attaining Peace" (*PI* 86).

8. We should note here that a script Frederick wrote for Annabel reminded her of James's novella.

9. Gaston Bachelard in his work *The Poetics of Space* refers to the "offensive capacity of shells. In the same way that there are ambush-houses, there exist trap-shells which the imagination makes into fish-nets, perfected with bait and snap" (125).

10. From the beginning of the text, we witness this change of appearance that follows every change of the image in Annabel. Thus, from the pale and unimpressive woman that she used to be as an unknown actress, she becomes the impressive, well-bred Lady-Tiger when she is famous.

11. This excerpt is from J. B. Robinet's *Vues philosophiques de la gradation naturelle des formes de l'être, ou les essais de la nature qui apprend a faire l'homme*, Amsterdam 1768.

12. According to the ancient myth, Narcissus was cursed by Echo to fall in love with his image and die of grief, because he mocked her love. The curse is realized and Narcissus falls for his reflection, which he sees in the calm waters of a pool: "He loves an unsubstantial hope and thinks that substance which is only shadow" (Ovid 153). From then on his life is a torment and he dies of grief for this love that can never be returned.

5

Gold Rush—Or, All That Glitters Is Gold in *The Takeover*

> If you can comprehend a morality devoid of ethics or civil law, this was
> really the guiding principle of both people.
>
> —Muriel Spark
> *Aiding and Abetting*

With *The Takeover* Muriel Spark writes an excitingly amoral novel about the
revival of paganism in the decade of the '70s in Italy, a country that is fascinated
with mother cults, beginning with mother goddesses of ancient religions and
ending in the cult of Mary, the mother of God. Spark's narrative, situated in the
"dense greenery" of the lake of Nemi near Rome, deconstructs all stable
construction immersing them in a hyperreal universe.

In this novel, more than in any other of Muriel Spark's novels, the reader
not only fails to find a moral center, but is given the option of viewing
Catholicism and its Fathers as a continuation of primitive religious structures,
since they all believe in the same god: money. Christianity, following the rules
of societies of the spectacle, presents its followers with modern rituals in order
to lure them into its structures. The Catholic Church presented in the novel
seems to have effaced God through its preoccupation with secular
(im)materiality. Thus, the absence of God is replaced by a presence (quest for
power/money) that proves to be the very epitome of absence. Hubert, the so-
called high priest of the cult of Diana, poses a challenge for the Catholic
structure, as he uses the same mechanisms to seduce the masses, thus setting up
an imaginary duel with the pope of the Roman Catholic Church.

The novel's center or point of departure is Frazer's *The Golden Bough*, one of the greatest anthropological texts of all times, a study of the prevailing structures of ancient religions, dominated by the figure of the powerful high priest of the cults, the "man-god" as Frazer calls him, the Father. The other major text that makes its presence strongly felt is Freud's *Totem and Taboo*—a text itself highly influenced by *The Golden Bough*—where Freud studies the ambiguous relation with the father in primitive cultures and presents the idea that a longing for the place of the father "constitutes the root of every religion" (209).

However, both texts seem to stress the fluidity of signification and the loss of origins. All religious structures share common elements, while the original signifier, the One, cannot be traced anywhere. What can be traced is the everlasting desire for power, which has underwritten all religions.

Muriel Spark uses these two text to serve the goal of the novel, which is to emphasize the seduction of (the) *gold*(en bough), the artificial sign par excellence, that seems to annul all structures. With this novel Spark presents us not only with the most amoral text of her work but also with a narrative about the seduction of money, which has no value in itself but is simply passed on. Everything is given an exchange value, and money circulates with its absent presence in the novel, as if in an orbit, moving within virtual space. Religion comes to participate in this seduction by annihilating the Father behind the spectacle, whereas the Law of the Father is revealed to be property, gold.

At the very beginning of the narrative there is a description of three houses in Nemi, which belong to Maggie Radcliffe, a wealthy American who used to be Hubert's protectress. As the narrator informs us: "At Nemi, that previous summer, there were three new houses of importance to the surrounding district. One of them was new in the strict sense: it had been built from the very foundations on cleared land where no other house had stood, and had been *planned*, *plotted*, *discussed* with an *incomprehensible* lawyer, and constructed, over a period of three years and two months" (*T* 5, italics added). The text, therefore, begins with a parody of property: the houses not only have to be "planned, plotted, discussed" as though they were narratives, but even as narratives, they are based on "incomprehensibility." Their very foundations, in other words, are unsteady. Property, it seems, like another language, has lost all stability and is moving within the realm of deconstruction. Although they are concrete parts of Maggie's fortune—a fact that will be disproved later—the houses are presented as mere fictions. Maggie, very much like her property, is also quite unspecified, an "indestructible" (*T* 7) presence based on absence. She is difficult to pin down but takes some time to materialize: "Maggie herself was never there that previous summer, was reputed to be there, was never seen, had been, had gone, was coming soon, had just departed for Lausanne, for London" (*T* 5).

With the description of the other two houses, the narrator closes the circle of themes of the novel, since we are presented with the concept of succession, where one construction is laid upon another: "The other two houses were reconstructions of buildings already standing or half-standing: both had foundations of Roman antiquity, and of earlier origin *if you should dig down far enough*, it was said" (*T* 5, italics added). Everything, then, points to another construction, in the same way that every signified, in the poststructural game, becomes another signifier in the endless game of signification.

Similar to the foundations of the houses, one cult is a continuation of the previous one as people seem to find through religions a way to manipulate the masses and make fortunes. In the novel there are allusions to the cult of the witches,[1] the cult of Diana, the cult of Apollo, and finally Christianity, mainly through Catholicism and particularly its modern charismatic phase. The novel is replete with references to all these layers of religions and their representative works through allusions to Freud's *Totem and Taboo*, Frazer's *The Golden Bough*, and the Bible. All the mythology around these religions is foregrounded, along with Hubert's effort to create a new mythology—based on the fictional constructs that preceded him—in which to situate himself.

All these interrelations of religions in *The Takeover* perplex the reader, who is lost in this dense web of myths. Frazer's attempt to trace the origins of the ritual of the Diana cult in Nemi seems to fail, as the Father (it was definitely a Father again) who first imposed this rule in the cult of Diana, the goddess of fertility, is lost in mythology. It could be Orestes or it could be Caligula, who first introduced the rite. The origins are lost or ambiguous; it seems as if any attempt to trace origins and Fatherhoods—in the many that we will see till the end of the novel—is vain. As John Vickery explains in his work *The Literary Impact of* The Golden Bough:

The Golden Bough contributed to this sense of the ongoingness of time and to the expectation of novelty even though it was consciously directed to showing how the present is determined by the past, how the uniqueness of Christianity is dissolved in its emergence from primitive fertility cults. As we watch the seemingly endless round of dying and reviving gods move across Frazer's pages, time, history, and human life appear to be on the verge of being drawn into a static cycle. Frazer did find the meaning of the present in the past and seems to imply that *true novelty is ultimately impossible*. (26, italics added)

One Father points to another, and one cult is associated with another so that we lose sight of the beginning, of the origin—if there ever was such a thing. Even Diana, the goddess of fertility or Mother Earth, is not the Origin; she originated from the Father of the Greek pantheon, Zeus the king of the gods of Olympus, who was the son of Kronos and Rea and so on.

Hubert's attempt to give his fatherhood a "historical" foundation—by claiming descent from the union of Caligula and Diana—is clearly (and even by him) mocked; its fictionality is foregrounded throughout the following passage:

But how, Hubert would demand of his listeners, did the mad Emperor Caligula have sex with a statue? It was an orgy on a lake-ship: there must have been something more than a statue. Caligula took Diana aboard his ship under her guise as the full moon, according to Suetonius. Diana the goddess, Hubert explained, was adept at adding years to the life of a man—she had done it with her lover Hippolytus. She bore a child to the madly enamoured Emperor, added years to the infant's life so that he became instantly adult, and it was this young man, and not a Roman hireling, whom Caligula sent to supplant the reigning King of the Wood, the priest of Diana.

Hubert descended, then, from the Emperor, the goddess, and from her woodland priest; in reality this was nothing more than his synthesis of a persistent, yet far more vague, little story fostered by a couple of dotty aunts enamoured of the author-image of Sir James Frazer and misled by one of those quack genealogists who flourished in late Victorian times and around the turn of the century, and who still, when they take up the trade, never fail to flourish. (*T* 41–42)

This, then, would seem to be the genealogy of the plot of the novel: the ancient historians' narrative that inspires Frazer's narrative that inspires Muriel Spark's narrative and the aunts' narrative that inspires Hubert's narrative and so on. People, enamored with myths and images, descendants of these myths and images, are the marks on the page and want to remain so, rather than become flat "reality."

Muriel Spark, in a deft ironic shift, turns the narrative that presumably inspired Frazer to write his "stories" and her to write her novel into Hubert's inspiration for his outrageous claims to descent from Caligula and Diana. This issue of descend from the union between the goddess and the emperor suggests the union between the virgin woman and God that resulted in the birth of Christ. Hubert, like Christ, is the fatherly son and husband of the virgin Mother Earth: Father of the cult, son because he was born from the union of Diana and Caligula, and husband since his priesthood gives him direct access to the phallus which is the goddess.[2] Moreover, this union between the goddess and the emperor evidently refers to the marriage between secular and religious authority, since Hubert is trying to imitate the pope's dual power.

Throughout the novel we experience the timelessness of the battle among fathers for the domination of one, as "The rule of the Phallus is the reign of One, of Unicity" (Gallop 66). Significantly, Spark places in the beginning of her narrative a rather long quote from "The King of the Wood," the first chapter of *The Golden Bough*, which is about the high priest of the cult of Diana of Nemi:

In the sacred grove grew a certain tree round which at any time of the day, and probably far into the night, a grim figure might be seen to prowl. In his hand he carried a drawn sword, and he kept peering warily about him as if at every instant he expected to be set upon by an enemy. He was a priest and a murderer; and the man for whom he looked was sooner or later to murder him and hold the priesthood in his stead. Such was the rule of the sanctuary. A candidate for the priesthood could only succeed to office by slaying the priest, and having slain him, he retained office till he was himself slain by a stronger or craftier." (J. G. Frazer as quoted in *T* 40–41)

Fathers or prospective fathers fight for the possession of the sword, the symbol that represents immediate access to the goddess, like the Lacanian father and son who fight over the possession of the phallic mother (a Lack), a stage that marks the child's entrance into the Symbolic. Evidently, it is the sword/phallus (an arbitrary symbol, actually an absence) that gives the power of Logos; the moment one becomes owner of the sword he immediately imposes his logos on others. As Jane Gallop explains in *Thinking Through the Body*; "[The Lacanian phallus] is neither a real nor a fantasized organ but an attribute: a power to generate meaning" (125–126). Thus, it is the control of this absence (the phallus/sword) that will grant man mastery over another absent structure (language).

Hubert manages to get possession of the phallus using the power of language. He crowns himself "King of Nemi" and becomes the King, the high priest; his words have the power to give him the sword in the eyes of his public, as we discover from the beginning of the narrative, through a discussion between Maggie and Mary, her daughter-in-law:

"Do you believe in the evil eye?" said Maggie still speaking very low.

"Well, no," said Mary whispering back in concert, "I believe I don't." She bent closer to Maggie.

"It's possible," Maggie breathed, "that if there is such a thing, Hubert has the evil eye. His name, Mallindaine, is supposed to be derived from an old English form, 'malline' which means of course malign, and 'Diane' with the 'i' and the 'a' reversed. He told me once, and as he explained it, the family reversed those syllables as a kind of code, because of course the Church would have liquidated the whole family if their descent from the pagan goddess was known. And they always worshipped Diana. It was a stubborn family tradition, apparently." (*T* 38)

Hubert, through his name, becomes the "evil eye,"[3] constructing his own fatherhood. Hubert manipulates language in order to give himself an identity, as we can see that his power resides in the presence of the goddess in his name. This idea takes us again to Freud's *Totem and Taboo*, where he comments on the savage's relationship with names and the process of naming:

[T]he savage looks upon his name as an essential part and an important possession of his personality, and he ascribes the full significance of things to words. . . . Numerous peculiarities of normal behaviour may lead civilized man to conclude that he too is not yet as far removed as he thinks from attributing the importance of things to mere names and feeling that his name has become peculiarly identified with his person. (75)

Hubert, however, goes one step further and un-names/re-names himself, thus creating a new personality, refusing to conform to any form of conditioning. In a playful mood, he explores fixed identities and linguistic structures. Moreover, he goes on to establish his existence on the absent presence of some documents, which finally lead to the falsity of his claims, when Pauline Thin, his secretary, after reading some of them finds "that something was amiss between Hubert's claims and the facts" (*T* 106). These antitheses, however, do not apply to Hubert as he hastens to suggest in a postmodern statement: "'Truth . . . is not literally true. Truth is never the whole truth. Nothing but the truth is always a lie . . .'" (*T* 106). In his speech Hubert refuses to accept the definition of concepts through their antithesis to other concepts. For him there seems to be coexistence and identification in antithesis. The same is suggested by Nietzsche in *Beyond Good and Evil*, where he poses the following questions: "How *could* something originate in its antithesis? Truth in error, for example? Or will to truth in will to deception? Or the unselfish act in self-interest? Or the pure radiant gaze of the sage in covetousness?" (33). One answer he gives is the following: "It might even be possible that *what* constitutes the value of those good and honoured things resides precisely in their being artfully related, knotted and crocheted to these wicked, apparently antithetical things, perhaps even in their being essentially identical with them" (34). In contrast to Pauline—obviously representing the Pauline doctrine in the novel—Hubert, like the novel itself, lies beyond such dichotomies between claims and facts, truth and lies, good and evil.

Hubert's language—despite its arbitrariness, or perhaps because of it—is highly seductive to his audience, contrary to the moral codes that Rodney Stenning Edgecombe imposes on the novel in his work *Vocation and Identity in the Fiction of Muriel Spark*, published in 1990, where he regrets the loss of certain attributes in Spark's fiction. As the following excerpt shows, Edgecombe insists on having captured the "author's position," which should have remained unchanged throughout her work. He feels disappointed at the "worthless" human beings Spark insists on presenting in her narratives: "Gone is the providential coda of judgement and reward that in, say, *Memento Mori* spelled out the author's position in relation to her characters. And gone also are a certain clarity and decisiveness. Having spent so much time imagining people as *worthless* as those of *The Takeover*, the author seems herself to have succumbed to their ennui and moral listlessness. Human beings now seem incorrigible, and the 'corrective' metaphysical framework that governed and shaped the early novels with such purposefulness has been dismantled" (113). The novel, it seems, refuses, like its characters, to conform to established conventions.

Along with all similar expectations that Spark, in her favorite technique, shatters in this novel, are also those for a "true" Father, not only through the narrator's continuous comments on Hubert's fictional nature but also through Hubert's ambivalent masculinity, which is interpreted in various ways by different characters throughout the text.[4] The following passage which comes in the beginning of the novel is highly revealing:

Hubert glanced back again at Pauline with her tiny face and her curly hair and felt the absence, now, of Ian, the boy from Inverness, and Damian, the Armenian boy with the curious surname of Runciwell who, as secretary, had been the best secretary, and he missed the other two with their petulance and their demands, their talents for cooking or interior design, their earrings and their neck-chains and their tight blue jeans and twin-apple behinds, fruit of the same tree. He felt their absence without specified regret; it was their kind he missed. (*T* 9)

The role of the Father in this narrative is given to the Other, or what is considered as the "outside" or "abnormal" of society. Spark inevitably leads the reader to the end of conventional fatherhood, as one cannot but wonder how this Other Father can be the One, Unicity. She initiates a new era of fatherhood, which draws its power from the old and "true" Fathers but which is so evidently a representative of the Other.[5]

Real or "foster" father, Hubert challenges the reign of the Father of Roman Catholicism by fighting with the same weapons. Throughout the narrative there is a battle in process—at least in Hubert's mind—between the high priest of the Diana cult, the first Pontifex, and the high priest of Catholicism, the pope, the other Pontifex.[6] Hubert, impressed by the masses attracted by the pope, desires to lure similar crowds in order to establish his cult and increase his property:

What Hubert had in mind for his final project was to try to syphon off, in the interests of his ancestors Diana and her twin brother Apollo, some of the great crowds that had converged on Rome as pilgrims for the Holy Year, amongst whom were vast numbers of new adherents to the Charismatic Renewal movement of the Roman Catholic Church. News had also come to Hubert of other Christian movements which described themselves as charismatic, from all parts of Europe and America; a Church of England movement, for instance, and another called the Children of God. Studying their ecstatic forms of worship and their brotherly claims it seemed to him quite plain that the leaders of these multitudes were encroaching on his territory. He felt a burning urge to bring to the notice of these revivalist enthusiasts who proliferated in Italy during the Holy Year that they were nothing but schismatics from the true and original pagan cult of Diana. It infuriated him to think of the crowds of charismatics in St Peter's Square, thumbing their guitars, swinging and singing their frightful hymns while waiting for the Pope to come out on the balcony. Not far from Nemi was the Pope's summer residence in Castelgandolfo. Next month, he fumed, they will crowd into Castelgandolfo, and they should be here with me. (*T* 147)

In this passage we have a one-to-one analogy between Hubert's cult and Catholicism, or what seems to be the pope's cult. The pope, as we gather from the passage, does not differ much from Hubert, staging his own fatherhood, through his "charismatic" followers, as Hubert will do later on in the novel. One spectacle is built upon another; one Father is staged on the other's performances. Through these charismatic celebrations for the Fathers, we witness the disappearance of God. The pope, who "has become the best special effect of the late twentieth century" according to Jean Baudrillard (*Cool Memories*, 146), seems to have taken the place of the One Father, since *he* is now the symbol of worship. Christianity, as Hubert suggests, resorts to primitive cults that laid special emphasis on the spectacle by performing impressive rites, in order to draw these crowds. As modern society depends so much on the power of the image, religion has to follow the trend and reproduce, simulate ancient rituals.

The reader, then, is made fully aware of this mythmaking process of constructing religions. Hubert is subjected to the preexisting language of the cult of Diana, to which he has to conform if he wants to establish himself as a Father of an old-new religion. However, he also has to follow the discourse that Catholicism has established through its imitation of primitive cults. Again based on a simulation of the simulation, he decides to reproduce a gathering, based on the information he has about the charismatic gatherings of the Catholic Church, which follow the structure of the witches' covenants, ancient Dionysian orgies, or who knows what else? Hubert's gathering is a reproduction of a Catholic gathering that Pauline attended and narrated to him.

Everything is moving on the realm of the hyperreal, the realm of simulations. One fiction is built upon another, and there is nothing to prove the "reality" of things. As Hubert states in a discussion with his secretary, Pauline, and two Jesuits: "'If you imagine . . . that appearances may belie the reality, then you are wrong. Appearances *are* reality. . . . In spite of what your religion claims, I say that even your religion is based on the individual perception of appearances only. Apart from these, there is no reality'" (*T* 72–73).

And what is the role of all these hyperreal simulacra but the attraction of the masses and the accumulation of money? As is evident from the above passage, Hubert realizes that he must satisfy people's need for "truth," not only through words—in the form of speech or writing—but also through stage management. (Nietzsche in *Beyond Good and Evil* claims "It is no more than a moral prejudice that truth is worth more than appearance; it is even the worst-proved assumption that exists" [61].) We encounter, in other words, a return to the power of the spectacle that was discussed in the previous chapter, a spectacle that is fabricated through Hubert's "evil eye" and is essential for the construction of his fatherhood. As he exclaims during one of his fights with Pauline: "'I've had experience with the theatre, I've had a lot of success, and when I ran my play in Paris, *Ce Soir Mon Frère*, I took responsibility for all the costumes'" (*T* 153). It is this imposing gaze and his well-staged presence that make sense out of non-sense.

First, Hubert uses the spoken word to create himself through creating his ancestors; then he resorts to writing to establish his identity, as written documents are necessary to prove "his-story," and he ends up in the power of the eye, staging himself in order to maintain his false identity. His constructs engulf the masses with their power of deception. Like Annabel in *The Public Image*, and like so many other characters in Spark's work, Hubert imposes his gaze on his viewers: "Hubert, splendid as a bishop *in pontificalibus*, folded in his vestments of green and silver, proceeded up the aisle giving his benediction to right and left" (*T* 107). Hubert is the eye that bends "severely" on others and kills their gaze.

The construction of images, not only through language but also through the careful staging of his presentations, plays a significant role in fabricating Hubert's fatherhood, as well as other fatherhoods—as Spark insinuates—in the novel. The Logos that God is supposed to have created is not enough because people want more than an absent presence to believe in a religion, since modern societies are dominated by the power of simulations. The simulacrum hides the absence of the thing, thus creating a false impression of something concrete. The charismatic renewal in the Roman Catholic Church testifies to people's need for presence, their inability to believe only with abstract words found on a page or uttered by a person.

Hubert, realizing this need for a presence through these charismatic gatherings, decides to return to the old rituals of his cult and organize for a few members of the Fellowship a secret meeting, which will "be held in the large overgrown garden behind the house stretching to the dark, moist woods" (*T* 152). They seem to have chosen the right place, the heart of the Mother Goddess, or rather her "dark" and "moist" reproductive organs. All the people who gather in the garden, like those who gather in the charismatic meetings of the Catholic Church, have the intention of simulating an orgy that will bring forth a sort of liberation, which, however, leaves everything empty and void. As Baudrillard points out in *The Transparency of Evil*, "Now all we can do is simulate the orgy, simulate liberation. We may pretend to carry on in the same direction, accelerating, but in reality we are accelerating in a void, because all the goals of liberation are already behind us, and because what haunts and obsesses us is being thus ahead of all the results—the very availability of all the signs, all the forms, all the desires that we had been pursuing" (3–4). The reader, like the participants in the orgy, is always found in the core of the void, the already said, the already experienced. Everything is a mere repetition, an imitation of a past action, a past word, a past work.

Hubert dresses in his "shiny and green robes," playing the role of the father, but Pauline—standing again for the Church of Rome—is unable to understand the "true" meaning of the cult and, playing for one more time the role of the primal sinner, destroys the effect of the meeting: "[Pauline was dressed in] a khaki cotton trouser-suit with metal-gold buttons on the coat and its four pockets; Pauline had tucked the trouser-legs into a pair of high canvas boots, so that the whole dress looked like a safari suit. The hunting effect was increased by a pale straw cocked hat which perched on her short curled hair" (*T* 152). Sartorial symbols are manipulated to speak the effects, but Pauline, associated as she is with the sterile aspect of Catholicism, misuses them. As Hubert exclaims in a moment of fury: "That woman has no sense of stage management. Tell her to go and remove those objectionable clothes. She's supposed to be the chief of Diana's vestals and she looks like Puss-in-Boots at the pantomime" (*T* 153). Unable to come to terms with the old religion, Pauline remains in her restricted domain, in her language, which denies and defies Hubert's attempt to rejuvenate the old rites.

It is not only Hubert's performance that is destroyed, but his Fatherhood as well. Pauline takes over "his" Bible, as the old slaves took over a branch from the sacred tree of Diana to challenge the King, and makes the first step toward challenging Hubert's priesthood. Hers is the challenge of the book as "Christianity is a religion of the book, and the West is a book culture. Like God, self, and history, the notion of the book is, in an important sense, theological" (Taylor 76). She reads from "his" book but she cannot understand, being outside the realm of the Symbolic. Pauline is so immersed in the existing structures that she can never really challenge them; her only objection is to the place that she has in these structures, as she is too ambitious to accept her servility. She conforms to Fatherhood and accepts Hubert as a true priest, but she wants a higher position within the given construction.

However, the above death is only a symbolic action, an enactment of the primitive rituals that represented the death and rebirth of the fertility god, who dies and is reborn to save the world from famine.[7] Like the fertility god, the lover of the goddess that he stands for, Hubert has to go through a ritualistic death and be reborn again the next day, symbolizing the death and rebirth of nature. Significantly and quite ironically it is Hubert's secretary (with her impossible desire to be his lover) who kills and resurrects him, as she arranges his transfer to the Catholic Church.

Again subjected to the structures of the charismatic meeting, Pauline "testifies" during Hubert's gathering, by reading from "'The First Epistle to Timothy, Chapter 1, Verses 3 and 4'" (T 158), which suggests that the cult of Diana of Ephesus was maintained because several people profited from it. Hubert, nevertheless, is determined to take over the Bible as well and make it really his-story, to alter the meaning of the words that Pauline read: "'And I say unto you,' crooned Hubert into the microphone, 'that Diana of Ephesus was brought to Nemi to become the great earth mother. Great is Diana of Nemi!'" (T 160). He is still the Father that can originate meaning.

It is another woman, Nancy, an English neighbor who completely destroys Hubert's fatherhood in his own play. She goes one step further from where Pauline left off and questions his construction itself: "'I want to say,' said Nancy, 'that the biblical passage you have heard is a condemnation of the pagan goddess Diana. It implies that the cult of Diana was only a silversmith's lobby and pure commercialism. Christianity was supposed to put an end to all that, but it hasn't. It—'" (T 161). This is then the hidden meaning behind all these mythologies and spectacles: pursuit of money and power/pursuit of an absence.

This climax is the moment of Hubert's symbolic death, brought forward from the women, Pauline, Nancy, and Letizia. However, in Christianity the death of the Son is a metaphor for the death of the body and the purification of the soul which is necessary for the entrance into the eternal world of God. As Kristeva comments in *Tales of Love* "Inhabited by Christ, 'adopted' by the Father, the believer puts to death only his sinful body, on the path that leads him to agape" (144). And she adds: "The killing of the body is the path through which the body-Self has access to the Name of the Other who loves me and makes of me a Subject who is immersed (baptized) in the Name of the Other" (146). As Hubert gains his fatherhood he is inserted into a long tradition of father murderers, who, through these murders, acquire eternal life, taking the place of their father, becoming father in his stead. This idea takes us to Freud's reference to the father complex, which was inherent in almost all religions and demanded the sacrifice of the father figure in the cult: "The original animal sacrifice was already a substitute for a human sacrifice—for the ceremonial killing of the father; so that, when the father-surrogate once more resumed its human shape, the animal sacrifice too could be changed back into a human sacrifice" (*Totem and Taboo* 213). In ancient Greece this started with Zeus and Kronos and continued in Christianity with Christ, who killed the absence of God and became the present God in His place.

Just at the point of the major climax in the novel, the Bible and Nancy finally touch on the one sign that governs all religious constructions: money, commercialism. Even if the quote remains unfinished, the message is clear: Christianity continues with this commercialism, by reproducing the spectacles that preceded it in an attempt to seduce the masses into its structures.

As all the action in the novel rotates around money, and all religions in the novel developed into a sheer camouflage in an effort to gain money, there is a constant interconnection between the two. Maggie herself can be read as a reincarnation of Diana, the triple goddess, who, in a parody of the myth, is reborn as a modern millionairess. The whole narrative is about the cult of Diana, the goddess with the triple nature as Manuela Dunn Mascetti informs us in her book *The Song of Eve*: "Diana-Artemis, Goddess of the Witches, was the Great Goddess of the legendary Amazons. . . . Diana in this respect was the Queen of Heaven, the pure Huntress of the Moon and Protectress of wild animals. . . . Diana in her second aspect was Asiatic Artemis, the orgiastic and many-breasted Mother of All. . . . In her third form she was Hecate, Dark Goddess of the Night Sky, giver of plagues and sudden death" (53). Maggie, herself, the "gorgeous," ageless, "indestructible" millionairess, is an interesting parody of the Mother-Goddess, as the narrative stresses most of all her alliance with gold: "She had overdressed very tastefully, with a mainly-white patterned dress *brilliant* against her *shiny* sun-tan. Her hair was *silver*-tipped, her eyes large and *bright*. She had a *flood-lit* look up to her teeth" (30, italics added).

Through Maggie, this union of religion and money is made evident in the following passage where the world of economics and the world of religion are interchangeable. Maggie is after her lawyer and financial advisor, who fled with all her fortune, leaving no traces: "Maggie was in Switzerland intently but vaguely *hunting* Coco de Renault through the *woods* and *thickets* of the Zürich banks, of the Genevan financial advisory companies, the investment counselling services of Berne, and through the *wildwoods* of Zug where the computers whirred and winked unsleepingly in their walls" (*T* 138–139, italics added). The diction that should be associated with the cult of Diana (hunting, woods, thickets, wildwoods) is used as a metaphor for the world of money—banks, advisory companies, investment counseling services—where, significantly, money is an absence. Like the goddess/god who disappears behind modern and ancient rituals and images, money—the modern god—is lost in the dense network of all these structures that have eliminated all exchange value.

Everything in the narrative works with images, as I explained. The characters are desperately trying to maintain their world through the full exploitation of images, a replacement of the "real" by simulation. A sudden change seems to have taken place in the field of economics. Everything is moving on a virtual scale, as simulation seems to have prevailed. Baudrillard in *The Transparency of Evil* stresses that:

[T]his glaring reality of today cannot have the meaning it had in the classical or Marxist accounts. Its motor is neither the infrastructure nor the superstructure of material production, but rather the *destructuring* of value, the destabilization of real markets and economies and the victory of an economy encumbered by ideologies, by social science, by history—an economy freed from "Economics" and given over to pure speculation; a virtual economy emancipated from real economies (not emancipated *in reality*, of course: we are talking about *virtuality*—but that is the point, too: today, power lies not in the real but in the virtual); and an economy which is *viral*, and which thus connects with all other viral processes. (34)

The narrator informs us of this change in economics—which took place in 1973, starting from the American Secretary of State, "a change in the meaning of property and money" (T 90)—and introduces us into this new "virtual economy" of "recession and inflation, losses in the stock-market, . . . the mood of the stock market, the health of the economy" (T 90–91). The following passage is indicative of the narrator's position toward these changes, whereby the absence of economics infects the realm of the "real": "They talked of hedges against inflation, as if mathematics could contain actual air and some row of hawthorn could stop an army of numbers from marching over it. They spoke of the mood of the stock-market, the health of the economy as if these were living creatures with moods and blood. And thus they personalized and demonologized the abstractions of their lives, believing them to be fundamentally real, indeed changeless" (T 90–91).

Like most other concrete things in Spark's work, money has also been replaced by its image. Nevertheless, this does not seem to hinder the characters who spend themselves in a continuous rotation around this signifier, which so lures them with its glitter. According to Baudrillard:

There is something much more shattering than inflation . . . and that is the mass of floating money whirling about the Earth in an orbital rondo. Money is now the only genuine artificial satellite. A pure artifact, it enjoys a truly astral mobility; and it is instantaneously convertible. Money has now found its proper place, a place far more wondrous than the stock exchange: the orbit in which it rises and sets like some artificial sun. (*The Transparency of Evil* 33)

Maggie's property is a constant absence, that somehow never materializes. The narrative plays continuously with this idea of a global property, and the narrator often briefs the reader on the condition of Maggie's money: "Mysterious and intangible, money of Maggie's sort was able to take lightning trips round the world without ever packing its bags or booking its seat on a plane" (99). Rather than becoming more of a presence, as the plot progresses, Maggie's property vanishes completely. Hubert takes over her house and refuses to leave, changing the locks every week so that she cannot enter, replacing her genuine antiques with fakes, as the possession of the sword and his fatherhood signify access to property. His immersion into the structure of the cult means that he can manipulate the goddess's property: "The drawing-room furniture was Louis XIV; there had been six fine chairs, at present only five; one was away in a clever little workshop on the Via di Santa Maria dell'Anima in Rome, being sedulously copied. Hubert was short of money, and, almost certain that Maggie would at least succeed in removing the furniture from the house, he was taking reasonable precautions for his future" (*T* 21).

Especially from the time Coco de Renault, the lawyer, takes charge of Maggie's fortune, it becomes a total absence, which cannot be traced anywhere. The text again completely undermines the role of the Law's absence. Instead of supporting order and structure, the representatives of the Law throw everything into an everlasting disorder and de-construction. Even the offices that carried out the administration of the fortune's absence are eliminated: "[Maggie] realized that her administration headquarters, which previously occupied an entire floor of offices in a New York block, with three full-time lawyers, twelve accountants and a noisy number of filing clerks and secretaries who fell silent on the few occasions that Maggie made a visitation thereupon, was now all disbanded" (*T* 100). Indeed, Maggie's property is manipulated as though it does not exist. It changes hands, goes from one part of the earth to another without ever finding stability, until at some point she completely loses "sight" of it.

Even concrete constructions are said to be absent, nonexistent. When Lauro, Maggie's servant, discovers in some old and forgotten papers that the land where Maggie's house is built belongs to his future wife, her lawyer comments: "[The house] does not exist. How can it exist? It is not on the records. In Italy if a house is not on the records, it has been constructed illegally and we call it *abusivo*. An *abusivo* construction does not exist in legal terms. . . . You don't exist when you inhabit a house that is *abusivo*" (*T* 136–137). The house, like the myths it was built on and like its inhabitants, is also a fiction, an absence. All entities in this narrative are incorporated in this *mise en abyme* of fictions, which, as they are uncovered one by one, always leave another fiction underneath until the reader is lost in this whirlpool of nonentities.

As is evident from the above quote, the law can prove the non-existence of a house. But what is the law in the novel, if not the very foundation of simulations, the cornerstone of hyperreality? Who does the law serve, other than the Law of the Father, which in this narrative is money, as I explained in the beginning of this chapter? Significantly, Maggie's three lawyers are presented as impostors who aim only at cheating her, robbing her of all her property. They all set up a camouflage of spectacles in order to cover their "true" identity, which is never revealed. They remain fictions to the end, absences who materialize only for a short time through their mythologies, and then again disappear when they have attained their law: money.

The first "incomprehensible" lawyer, with the significant name Dante de Lafoucault, is the one who sells Maggie the land at Nemi; but in the course of things it is discovered that "The whole of the transaction had been a fake, including the documents, and the land presumed to have been Church property belonged to Lauro's prospective bride at this moment" (*T* 135). Dante de Lafoucault, as his name suggests, is completely immersed in his fictitious documents. The second, Massimo de Vita, "the obscure lawyer whom Maggie had engaged to evict Hubert from his house" (*T* 126), becomes Hubert's ally and finally departs "for elsewhere" after selling all Maggie's furniture with Hubert and getting his half share: "Massimo had left for some unknown destination; he had said California, which meant, certainly, elsewhere; evidently he was used to departing speedily for elsewhere from time to time" (*T* 184). And the last one, Coco de Renault, who is in charge of Maggie's property as I explained above, disappears with Maggie's money. As she states: "'Coco de Renault has *completely* disappeared with all my money'" (168). The key word here is "completely," which further emphasizes Coco's absent presence throughout the narrative. From an occasional absence, which Maggie is constantly trying to locate all over the world,[8] Coco becomes a permanent one, simultaneously relieving Maggie of another occasional major absence, her money, which until then had been appearing in monthly checks.

In this realm of the hyperreal, where everything disappears behind its image, even threat will have to be simulated in order for a "real" threat to be prevented and for the existing structure to maintain its power. As Baudrillard suggests in *Simulations*: "It would take too long to run through the whole range of operational negativity, of all those scenarios of deterrence which, like Watergate, try to regenerate a moribund principle by simulated scandal, phantasm, murder—a sort of hormonal treatment by negativity and crisis" (36). Following this concept Maggie, when she finds a girl trespassing on her property, hires five private coast guards who, "dressed up as 'intruders'" (*T* 81), are supposed to keep "real" intruders away from her property. However, once the characters reach this stage, who can tell the "simulated" from the "real"? Maggie's coast guards are intruders, no matter if they are "real" or not.

Simulations, then, become the armory of the capital. It is through the power of the simulacrum that they try to protect their construction. "'The time is coming,' Maggie said severely, 'when we'll have to employ our own egg-throwers to throw eggs at us, and, my God, of course, miss their aim, when we go to the opera on a gala night'" (*T* 81). This idea is again stressed by Baudrillard in *Simulations*: "Power can stage its own murder to rediscover a glimmer of existence and legitimacy. Thus the American presidents: the Kennedys are murdered because they still have a political dimension. Others—Johnson, Nixon, Ford—only had a right to puppet attempts, to simulated murders. But they nevertheless needed that aura of an artificial menace to conceal that they were nothing other than mannequins of power" (37).

However, the continuous coexistence of simulation and the real leads to a final embrace of the two, when at some point even the capital falls into its own trap. Maggie's husband Berto comes to believe in the threat of the Communists who are going to rob him of his property. The Communists become "They," the distant danger that looms over their heads. However, the narrator plays with Berto's fear, as the following excerpt suggests: "The Communists became 'They', the Italian '*Loro*'. Berto said, '*Loro, loro, loro* . . . They, they . . .'" (*T* 144). This distant threat, then, is "loro." But what is that "loro"? Isn't it gold itself? The Italian word for gold is "l'oro." Isn't this a hint that Berto's real weakness is his strength, that the threat lies in his own structure rather than with the Communists? It is not "they" that pose the threat, but "it": gold, money, the sign that Berto identifies with, the capital that he represents. As Berto's friend Emilio states: "'After the capitalists have finished with us I doubt if there will be anything left for the Communists to take over'" (*T* 144). Their money in the end is taken by its protectors, its manipulators. It is Maggie herself who appoints Coco de Renault responsible for her property, as she wants to participate in the newly emerging globalization of money. And when she realizes the complete absence of her lawyer and her money, she decides to take action.

However, she is more and more immersed in games of simulation. Since her money has always been an absence, nothing changes in her life when it "completely" disappears. As the narrative suggests, she is still as glamorous and radiant as ever. Therefore, she has to simulate her poverty: "'I dressed up as a pauper, . . . because I am a pauper. I am ruined. I just wanted everyone to know'" (*T* 181). She masquerades as a pauper in clothes that she buys from a secondhand store: "[a] worn-out long skirt of black cotton, a pair of soiled tennis shoes . . . , a once-pink head scarf, a cotton blouse, not second-hand but cheap, piped with white, and terrible" (*T* 179). The problem for her is that again appearances are taken for reality. When Maggie attempts to get into her house she is caught by the police, and she ends up "handcuffed to two burly carabinieri" (181).

There is another character who accumulates a considerable property by the end of the novel. Everything seems to have worked perfectly for Lauro who ends up with the houses in Nemi and a great part of Maggie's property. But who is Lauro and what does he stand for in this novel that is replete with parodies? What else could he stand for but for what his name signifies: gold, "l'oro," that

Berto mentions in relation to the Communists, the distant, non-existent threat that will come out of nowhere, when ironically Lauro/l'oro is in the same house with him.[9] Lauro, then, gets to take everything in the end, through his marriage to a woman he despises but marries willingly, as her family presents him with the documents that prove their (and later his) possession of the land of Nemi.

Lauro is highly charismatic, presented as an all-body presence who has the power to satisfy everyone—man or woman—sexually, desired by all but never possessed. Lauro—who has sex with Hubert, Maggie, her son Michael, her daughter-in-law Mary, her husband Berto, the maid and others, steals money and performs all kinds of atrocious actions in the novel—is the perfect representation of gold. Naturally, the presence of gold alone is capable of sexually arousing Lauro, as the reader can realize from the erotic scene between Lauro and Mary: "The sight of so much *golden* money in the *rich, very rich*, tall girl's hands *inflamed* him instantly with sexual desire. He grabbed the box and pulled her into the thick green glade. He pulled her down to the ground and with the box spilling beside them he would have raped her had she not yielded after the first gasp" (47, italics added).

If we see Lauro in religious terms—since gold and religion are constantly associated in the novel—he seems to be the "fatherly son" of Mother Earth. The following scene where he hides some of the gold coins that Maggie had given him for Hubert, in his mother's "bosom," or in the soil of her grave is highly symbolic:

Lauro, on his knees, dutifully d[ug] and tend[ed] his mother's flower-bed. . . . When he had dug enough and laid on the grass verge some of the flowers and plants he had dislodged in the process, he opened up the sheets of newspaper which contained the black leather box. . . . He opened the box, lifted the paper-tissues which he had stuffed inside to keep the coins from rattling, sifted a few of the beautiful golden disks through his brown fingers, quickly replaced the lot, put the black box in the orange plastic bag for safe preservation and, seeing that it was well-covered, he buried it deep. On the top of this he replaced some of the short shrubs he had dug up.

He began also to plant the new chrysanthemum roots he had brought, working his way around the grave. . . . . While he was at it he dug up, examined, and replaced two well-wrapped little parcels, one containing a huge sapphire ring and the other a pair of monogrammed cuff-links, these being objects he had picked up somewhere along the line from two earlier periods and encounters in his young life. (*T* 55–56)

Lauro always goes back to the mother's body, sharing with her a love relationship, where money is the mediator, as it is the central issue of the whole novel. He puts his gold in the mother's bosom in an attempt to valorize it, as in itself it has no value. And the mother pays up; he finally becomes the goddess's heir, since she gives him all her land.

He ends up being the King of the Wood, Dianus or Janus, Diana's lover,[10] and Maggie his Goddess who shares her fortune with him when he helps her kidnap Coco de Renault and hide him in the caves around the lake of Nemi until

Coco's wife pays the ransom. For one more time, "gold" is buried in the bowels of the goddess and it has to pay up.

Once more lost in their simulations, Maggie as the wise witch, and Hubert as the high priest of the charismatic phase of Catholicism this time, go on their way rejoicing—to remember a favorite phrase of Spark's. "[Maggie] said good night very sweetly and, lifting her dingy skirts, picked her way along the leafy path, hardly needing her flash-lamp, so bright was the moon, three-quarters full, illuminating the lush lakeside and, in the fields beyond, the kindly fruits of the earth" (*T* 189). The moon is "bright" and the "fruits of the earth" are there awaiting any challengers who might be interested in possessing or being possessed by the modern god/goddess, whose presence through the moon and the lush vegetation cannot be disputed:

Our long voyage of discovery is over and our bark has drooped her weary sails in port at last. Once more we take the road to Nemi. It is evening, and as we climb the long slope of the Appian Way up the Alban Hills, we look back and see the sky aflame with sunset, its golden glory resting like the aureole of a dying saint over Rome and touching with a crest of fire the dome of St. Peter's. The sight once seen can never be forgotten, but we turn from it and pursue our way darkling along the mountain side, till we come to Nemi and look down on the lake in its deep hollow, now fast disappearing in the evening shadows. The place has changed but little since Diana received the homage of her worshippers in the sacred grove. The temple of the sylvan goddess, indeed, has vanished and the King of the Wood no longer stands sentinel over the Golden Bough. But in the west, there comes to us, borne on the swell of the wind, the sound of the church bells of Rome ringing the Angelus. *Ave Maria!* Sweet and solemn they chime out from the distant city and die lingeringly away across the wide Campagnan marshes. *Le roi est mort, vive le roi! Ave Maria!* (Frazer 714)

NOTES

1. Witchcraft, for example, is at the core of this novel, as it is the fertility cults of Diana to which the origins of witches used to be traced. Mircea Eliade informs us in his work *Occultism, Witchcraft and Cultural Fashions* that "the charges of witchcraft attested to in northern Italy do not speak of adoration of the Devil but of the cult of Diana" (75). The cult remained a very strong influence for centuries, even after the prevalence of Christianity, because its practices were considered necessary for the prosperity of the community. In this work Eliade quotes a long excerpt from Elliot Rose's *A Razor for a Goat*, "a close analysis and a devastating, though humorous, criticism of [Dr. Murray's] theory" (72). Dr. Margaret Murray, an Egyptologist, was a very influential theoretician whose book *The Witch-Cult in Western Europe* (1921) made a major impact on the theory of witchcraft. In her work she claimed that the witch was a member of the cult of Janus or Dianus, a two-faced, horned god, who is described in *The Golden Bough* as Diana's lover. This "two-faced, horned god, identifiable with Janus or Dianus" cannot fail to bring to mind Spark's novel *The Ballad of Peckham Rye*, where Dougal Douglas, or Douglas Dougal, well known in the community for the two bumps of his head, possesses unique powers of changing personalities, as if he were the main protagonist in a continuous process of wearing different masks in order to enchant his public. While he is speaking

with Mr. Druce, one of his employers, these masks succeed one another at tremendous speed, catching their victim unawares. Dougal Douglas, or Douglas Dougal, or even Dougal-Douglas is the two-horned demon with the deformed shoulder from Edinburgh who manages to bring chaos out of order, evil out of morality, who manages to overturn the whole community of Peckham with his influence. His friend Humphrey Place is so dis-placed by Dougal's presence that he refuses his bride at the altar, using almost the exact words Dougal had used in a sarcastic imitation of the situation in front of Humphrey: "Dougal read from the book: 'Wilt thou take this woman,' he said with a deep ecclesiastical throb, 'to be thai wedded wife?' Then he put the plate aside and knelt; he was a sinister goggling bridegroom. 'No,' he declared to the ceiling. 'I won't, quite frankly'" (*BPR* 112). The actual scene of the marriage ceremony, which precedes Dougal's in the novel but succeeds it chronologically, is as follows: "The vicar said to Humphrey, 'Wilt thou have this woman to thy wedded wife?' 'No,' Humphrey said, 'to be quite frank I won't'" (*BPR* 8). Mr Druce, Dougal's employer acquires, under the latter's influence, a peculiar attraction to bottle openers, knives, paper knives until he finally murders his lover with a corkscrew. Druce's partner, Mr. Weedin, is so unbalanced by Dougal's similarities with the devil that he suffers a breakdown and is forced to leave the company: "Mr Weedin dropped his head on his hands. 'It may surprise you,' he said, 'coming from me. But it's my belief that Dougal Douglas is a diabolical agent, if not in fact the Devil. . . . Do you know that Douglas himself showed me bumps on his head where he had horns . . . Have you looked . . . at his eyes? That shoulder—'" (*BPR* 81–82). Merle Coverdale, Mr. Druce's lover and secretary, becomes quite restless in Dougal's presence: "'You've unsettled me, Dougal, since you came to Peckham'" (*BPR* 98).

2. Kristeva in *Tales of Love* explains that "according to a number of iconographic representations [of the Eastern Church], Mary can be seen changed into a little girl in the arms of her son who henceforth becomes her father. . . . Indeed, *mother* of her son and his *daughter* as well, Mary is also, and besides, his *wife*: . . . she therefore actualizes the threefold metamorphosis of a woman in the tightest parenthood structure" (243).

3. The idea of the "evil eye" is another recurrent theme in Spark's work. Closely associated with the cult of the witches, it is supposed to be an attribute of the witch—male or female—who can bring misfortunes to people simply by looking at them. In *Symposium*, Margaret represents the witch who can destroy with her "evil eye", as the following dialogue between Margaret and her mad uncle Magnus reveals: "How do you propose to rid yourself of Hilda Damien?' 'I will bide my time,' said Margaret. 'Perhaps your evil eye will be enough,' said Magnus. 'Only think about it, concentrate enough, and something will happen to her'" (*S* 159). Margaret is herself aware of her "evil eye," which has driven people to death. Her only desire is to participate actively in the disasters that her "evil eye" brings about: "'I almost think it's time for me to take my life and destiny in my own hands, and actively make disasters come about'" (*S* 143–144). Moreover, the main character's name—Margaret Murchie—and the novel's preoccupation with witchcraft could lead us to the wild guess that she alludes to Margaret Murray, the Egyptologist, who in 1921 wrote her famous work *The Witch-cult in Western Europe*.

4. Pauline describes Hubert as "a bit fagoty" to one of her friends, but at the same time she is highly attracted to him, sometimes perceiving him as a challenge, the man that no woman has ever had.

5. Spark does the same thing in her novel *The Abbess of Crewe* where the Father figure in the covenant is a woman, a female parody of President Nixon.

6. As we learn from Manuela Dunn Mascetti, the Christian pope's name "deriv[es] from the Latin term of address for the chief priest, *Pontifex* " (197).

7. Manuela Dunn Mascetti informs us that "The root of the mythology of the mother lies . . . in the ancient theme developed in Mesopotamia of the Mother Goddess who chooses a lover as the God of fertility. This lover dies periodically in self-sacrifice in order to save his people from famine and death. His body is buried and the god is born again as sprouting grain. The worship of the Great Mother of the Gods and her lover was very popular in the ancient world. Numerous similarities can be drawn between the ancient myths and the Christian tale of the Virgin Mary and Jesus Christ, so much so that the latter could be said to be an inheritance from the myths of the planters" (175).

8. The narrator continuously gives the reader information about Coco's disappearances and Maggie's frantic efforts to locate him. The following excerpt is an example of this process: "[I]n the hotel room [she] tried one number after another in search of Coco and her power of attorney. She tried San Diego, California, Port au Prince, Hong Kong, London, Zurich, Geneva and St Thomas in the Virgin Islands. The she tried Madras" (*T* 101).

9. The ideas for an association between Lauro and l'oro (gold), as well as for the link between Pauline and the Catholic Church were introduced by Professor Jina Politi.

10. As Sir James Frazer explains in *The Golden Bough*: "What little we know of the functions of Diana in the Arician grove seems to prove that she was here conceived as a goddess of fertility, and particularly as a divinity of childbirth. It is reasonable, therefore, to suppose that in the discharge of these important duties she was assisted by her priest, the two figuring as King and Queen of the Wood in a solemn marriage, which was intended to make the earth gay with the blossoms of spring and the fruits of autumn, and to gladden the hearts of men and women with healthful offspring" (163).

Epilogue

Memento Mori?

> There really does exist in the mind a compulsion to repeat which overrides the pleasure principle.
>
> —Sigmund Freud
> "Beyond the Pleasure Principle"

From what I have shown in this work, it is to death that Spark's fiction continuously returns; it is the call of *Memento Mori* that seduces her characters into an embrace with the caller. Whether they try to escape the calling or whether they rush toward it, they are left with no choice. The structure engulfs and drowns them.

Remaining faithful to the repetition compulsion that has led me all the way through this project, what would be a better idea than to turn briefly to Muriel Spark's *Memento Mori*, as a return to the seduction of death that has given life to my book.

Memento Mori reiterates over and over again this game of the lure of repetition. The caller's message seduces the old people in the narrative into this vicious circle of a return to death; one death succeeds another. There is a total of fifteen deaths in the novel, and the characters are consumed in an endless death talk—attending funerals, reading obituaries, or discussing the state of their "faculties"—until their moment comes to enter the circle of deaths when the caller knocks on their door.

The novel is a recitation of ages and abilities in the camp of the old, which suffocates the reader with its density. As fifteen out of the seventeen main characters in the novel are more than seventy years old, the narrative is naturally consumed in recounting, to the utmost detail, the deterioration of body and mind. The nightmarish cycle of death cannot be broken; it stays intact until the very end, leaving no doubts about its future continuation.

However, to follow the spirit of Muriel Spark's preoccupation with death, which reveals both an ending and a new beginning, I felt the need to open my epilogue with a brief discussion of Spark's latest novels.

REALITY AND DREAMS: A TRIP TO NO-MAN'S LAND

As this recent text, *Reality and Dreams,* focuses again on "textasy," the *jouissance* of signifiance, the industry of the spectacle, and the death brought by structures, it helps me foreground an openness, rather than a closure, by initiating a reading of this recent narrative.

Like most of Spark's works that insert her reader to a particular camp, this one introduces us into the camp of the redundant—redundancy evidently being a major form of death, where the structure, after having used its subjects, throws them out of its domain.

Like *The Public Image* that was discussed in detail in the third chapter, this novel places the action in the film industry, which once more dominates the scene. The narrative plays with the ideas of the power of the text and the image, the relationship between the author and the work, the merging of fiction and reality. Tom Richards, a famous film director and a scriptwriter, is longing for the old position of "authority" that he enjoyed in relation to his work. The old-fashioned crane that he insists on using in order to manipulate his actors without any external interferences, significantly represents the dominant presence of the Godlike author: "Yes, I did feel like God up on that crane. It was wonderful to shout orders through the amplifier and like God watch the team down there group and re-group as bidden. . . . Right up there I was beyond and above pausing a minute and listening to their suggestions. What do they think a film set is? A democracy, or something?" (*RD* 14). From his crane he "speaks" his subjects through his amplifier and kills them in his representations, while they willingly accept this role, this seduction of his structures.

However, things could not be as simple as that in a novel by Muriel Spark. One takeover succeeds another, as all the characters and all constructions enter the vicious circle of seduction and death. Tom, avenged for his Godlike dominance by his beloved construction—the crane—which throws him out, ends up in hospital with most of his bones broken (it is, after all, an old crane not fit for new use).

It is in the hospital that he has his dream, another version of his script, and things become complicated. Texts continuously overlap, to the point that one loses sight of the dividing lines between reality, script, dream, novel. The reader is never informed about how the characters come to know of Tom's dream-text which envelops them immediately. Jeanne, an actress who plays in the film the role of the "hamburger girl"—whom Tom saw for a moment in a camp in Paris and who inspired him for his recent film—is completely immersed in her dream-part; her reality is Tom's dream, where her presence is much more important than the minor part she has in the film: "Jeanne was an idea. A hamburger girl, frequently with her back to the camera, whose part in the story was by definition that of a nobody. 'But I,' insisted Jeanne, 'am the one who's going to inherit, to be a millionairess'" (*RD* 110).

Much as Tom wants to be God and "speak" his subjects, it is these subjects that end up directing him. It is not only that Jeanne, his dream girl, haunts him to the end of the narrative, trying to take from him the leading role in the construction of images. His life is completely immersed in his scripts; "'He lives films'" (*RD* 21) as his beloved daughter Cora suggests. His "reality" is undermined throughout the novel. Life is seduced into his scenarios, or vice versa. His second and repulsive daughter, Marigold, is referred to as his "conception" (*RD* 34). Once more in the steps of Mary Shelley's *Frankenstein*, Marigold is the monstrous creation which, as its creator is unable to explain it, must be eliminated: "Hideous Marigold. Always negative Marigold. Her parents searched through the past, consulted psychiatrists, took every moment to bits. In no way could she be explained" (*RD* 87).

This monstrous conception, however, does not hesitate to take action and get her revenge on her father who suggests that "She was always resentful of [his] dream" (*RD* 98). She decides to "walk off the scene" (*RD* 89) and chase her father through her absence in order to manipulate the narrative of his life: he is believed to be the murderer of his daughter, since nobody manages to trace her. Wandering all over the globe, she haunts him through his own dreams/scripts, past and present. First, she goes to the camp where he was inspired for his recent film and laughs at him unseen, when he goes to his dream-scenery to find her, but fails to notice her. Then, she haunts him in his new dream for another film about a prophet Celt in Roman Britain: "Tom couldn't sleep at nights. For a week he puzzled over the casting of Cedric the Celt. Night after night before his closed eyes, and practically on his pillow in the morning, looking at him, looking . . . he could see the dark sullen ugly face of Marigold, herself. 'I know of no star to resemble her,' he said to Claire, 'but she haunts my dreams as the Celt, Cedric the sorcerer'" (*RD* 132). Following an endless sequence of "takeovers," Marigold—imprisoned in her father's image of her in his dream, and as women are once again identified with appearances—is found disguised as a boy, ready to be killed in Tom's film. Cedric the sorcerer is "assassinated by superstitious zealots in the end," as "Tom thought Marigold would look well dead. . . . Marigold as Cedric the Celt lay finally with her eyes upturned, three daggers in her blood-stained tunic, and her lips forming a half-smile" (*RD* 143). The daughter's desire to kill the father, however, is no less strong; her plan to have the crane tampered with so that Tom is killed fails. In another turn of events, Jeanne, "the hamburger girl," dominates the finale by getting killed when she falls from the crane, which is evidently too dangerous a toy to be playing with. In this sequence of chases it is evident that power resides in absence. Only through their disappearance can the characters dominate the game of spectacles for a while, before they are seduced by their own or others' constructs.

The whole novel depicts the deferral of the desire to manipulate the structures where the characters find themselves trapped. They cannot escape the conditioning of these structures, as Tom cannot escape immersion in his own constructs, which, in turn, are enveloped within the novel, itself engulfed in the "script" form that it reflects. Ending where it all began, the narrative, very appropriately, closes with the characters' immersion "here in the tract of no-man's land between dreams and reality, reality and dreams" (*RD* 160).

AIDING AND ABETTING: A COMEDY OF ERRORS

> The fellow is distract, and so am I,
> And here we wander in illusions—
> Some blessed power deliver us from hence!
> —William Shakespeare
> *The Comedy of Errors*

This never-never land is to be found again in Spark's latest novel *Aiding and Abetting*. The dividing line between reality and fiction is never to be found in the text, which immerses the reader into an adventurous intertextual web made up of innumerable threads that lead, among others, to Shakespeare's *The Comedy of Errors*, Breuer and Freud's *Studies on Hysteria*, Beckett's *Waiting for Godot*, the New Testament, and real events.

The novel begins with a short reference by the author herself to the news story that actually initiated the narrative. It is the story of the seventh Earl of Lucan who murdered his children's nanny, battered his wife and then disappeared never to be found again. The Earl, as Spark informs us, "was declared officially dead in 1999, his body has never been found, although he has been 'sighted' in numerous parts of the world" (*AA* v).

Thus, it is after his death that the ghost of "Lucky" Lucan returns to haunt the readers and the narrative with his absent presence. This is actually a text initiated from an absence that was never traced, an empty signifier that always remains open, or rather refers to numerous other signifiers, refusing to close the circle of signification. As we are often informed in the novel, there have been sightings of Lucan, but it always proved to be somebody else, not the "real one."

As far as the Earl is concerned, things are quite clear; the author informs us about the "facts" of this story that has been significantly covered by the press, so we can always "trace" him to a certain extent. The problem is with the second main character in the novel, Dr. Hildegard Wolf, or Beate Pappenheim as her "real" name was. Her story is also "real," as Muriel Spark comments in her "Note to the Readers" that precedes the novel: "The parallel 'story' of a fake stigmatic woman is also based on fact" (*AA* vi). Spark does not bother to give us the details of this "stigmatic" woman. Who was she? When and where did she live? What was her story? Thus, the reader is partly left suspended as to the complete "facts" that lie behind the novel. Pappenheim/Wolf is actually more of an absence than a presence.

I tried to trace this "stigmatic," but the only "stigmata" that I found were the two names that she is given in the text: Dr. Wolf, her fake name, and Miss Pappenheim, her real name. These two "stigmata," however, are enough to betray her to a certain extent, but again they lead to a plethora of images. Her real name definitely alludes to the Freud/Breuer double and the very origins of psychoanalysis presented in their work *Studies on Hysteria*. Pappenheim was the real name of "Anna O.," the first "hysteric" to be treated by Breuer, who later became an active feminist. Pappenheim was the first to introduce the term "talking cure," the concept of transference, and the involvement of sexuality in neuroses. It was Anna O./Pappenheim who seduced and was seduced by the psychoanalyst (transference/countertransference); she forced him to face woman's sexuality and flee. Breuer abandoned the case horrified, when he found his "patient," as Stefan Zweig explains in a letter to Freud, "writhing in abdominal cramps. Asked what was wrong with her, she replied: 'Now Dr. B.'s child is coming!' . . . Seized by conventional horror he took flight and abandoned the patient to a colleague" (Forrester 17).

This dynamic "hysteric" finds her voice in this narrative, and returns to seize her doctors' power. Beate Pappenheim's ghost returns to haunt her former authors, by usurping their language. Beate as a medical student in her early twenties in Germany enters the structures of the Catholic Church, by pretending to be a stigmatic in order to gain money. When she is discovered, she flees Germany and ends up in Paris, where she becomes a famous psychoanalyst, changing her name to Dr. Hildegard Wolf. She discovers a magnificent new psychoanalytic technique, thus gaining the admiration of both public and colleagues, although she defies psychoanalysts' associations. Her technique, unlike the old psychoanalytic methods, forces the patient to hear the doctor's stories first, before being allowed to enter the stage of the "talking cure." This is definitely an interesting reversal of the doctor/patient role in psychoanalysis; it seems that the two are interchangeable in this game with psychoanalytic methods.

Her new name alludes to another famous persona in psychoanalysis, Freud's Wolf Man. Of course, in this case the Wolf is female, it is a Wolf Woman. This persona in Freud's work is another absence, hidden behind a fake signifier. Suffering from infantile trauma, the Wolf Man was lost in the images of his beloved—his sister and his father—that he carried within him, and which overpowered his own personality. Moreover, his fake name gave him another fictional persona that was different/other from his "reality." As Nicolas Abraham and Maria Torok very aptly put it, "This man, who is at once strange and average, has always lived under the guise of a double identity . . . . His friends do not know that for analysts his name is Wolf Man and, as for analysts, they do not know, save for a few, what his real name is. It is as if he has to maintain two separate worlds that cannot, must not communicate with each other" (30). Beate Pappenheim fits this model perfectly, because she, too, has to hide her "reality" from everyone around her. Beate Pappenheim is dead, another absence wanted by the police, but untraceable, a signifier that enjoys playing games with the absence of origins as is evident from the very first paragraph: "Dr. Hildegard Wolf, the psychiatrist who had come from Bavaria, then Prague, Dresden, Avila, Marseilles, then London, and now settled in Paris" (*AA* 1).

Papenheim/Wolf may come to haunt her-stories and psychoanalysis, however, the hidden "skeletons" of her past come to haunt her in the face of two men—or rather a master/slave double (very much like the Lucky/Pozzo double in *Waiting for Godot*)—who blackmail her with her illegal activities. Both men present themselves as "Lucky" Lucan, and they are interchangeable throughout the novel, despite the revelation of the "true" Lucan in Chapter 13 of the novel. Here, the allusion is to another text, Shakespeare's *The Comedy of Errors*, which focuses on a double again: two twin brothers are unaware of each other's presence, until they find themselves in the same town and turn from absences into presences. In Chapter 12, the narrator makes a direct reference to Shakespeare's comedy, when Hildegard cannot distinguish between the two Lucans: "The men were each, to her, 'a mere anatomy, a mountebank . . . a living-dead man,' as Shakespeare had put it long ago" (*AA* 124). This excerpt is from the last act in Shakespeare's play, and it refers to doctor Pinch, who diagnosed one of the twin brothers in the play as mad: "They brought one Pinch, a hungry lean-fac'd villain; / *A mere anatomy, a mountebank,* / A thread-bare juggler and a fortune-teller, / A needy-hollow-ey'd-sharp-looking-wretch; / *A living dead man*" (Shakespeare 99-100, italics added). This identification of the two Lucans with the ignorant doctor raises questions as to their identity. What is the role of the two men in Spark's novel? If they are the twins of the Shakespearean comedy, why are they identified—through this quote—with the doctor, who declares one of the twins mad? Could it be that in Spark's text, the two twins are the doctors of Pappenheim's past, who come back to reclaim their authority? They come as "anatomies"/skeletons of her past and threaten her with a revelation.

It would be interesting to note here that Bertha Pappenheim or Anna O. did indeed see skeletons, or "death's heads," according to Breuer's account, on two occasions: "While she was nursing her father she had seen him with a death's head. . . . As she came into the room, she had seen her pale face reflected in a mirror hanging opposite the door; but it was not herself that she saw but her father with a death's head" (Breuer and Freud 92). Dianne Hunter offers a very interesting interpretation of this last episode in her paper "Hysteria, Psychoanalysis and Feminism: The Case of Anna O.": "When she looked into the mirror she saw a death's head. Rejecting the cultural identity offered her, she tried to translate herself into another idiom. She regressed from the symbolic order of articulate German to the semiotic level of the body and the unintelligibility of foreign tongues" (100). Anna O. refused to conform to the patriarchal role for womanhood. Thus, she could not tolerate her reflection with her father's body and a death's head that signifies the role she has to play as the daughter of a Jewish Orthodox family. Her only outlet seems to be a violent reaction of the body, which will liberate her from her inert position and will allow her to reclaim her body, and give utterance to her narrative, her "private theater."

The Pappenheim of the novel proves to follow on her double's footsteps. She rejects the structure of her crowded and poor family, and becomes the rich saint, through the exploitation of her menstrual blood. As one of the characters admits toward the end of the novel: "I know she posed as a stigmatic. That I admire. I don't blame her for doing something constructive with her own blood. What else should a woman of imagination do with her menstrual blood?" (*AA* 158). Thus, she makes of her body a locus of signification, rich in symbolism; she resorts "to the semiotic level of the body" to be able to speak her difference. She manipulates signs, symbols, texts to achieve her purpose. Her body reiterates and plays with the idea of the catharsis brought by "the Blood of the Lamb," a phrase used repeatedly in the novel: "'[Blood] is not purifying,' she said, 'it is sticky. We are never washed by blood.' 'It is said we are washed in the Blood of the Lamb,' [Lucan] said, sticking his knife into lamb chop number three" (*AA* 38).

What is, then, this idea of blood-use in the novel? Whose is the blood and what purpose does it serve? The one certain thing is that for Beate Pappenheim it brought a liberation, because through that blood she managed to flee Germany and turn herself into a free signifier—not to mention the fact that, according to most witnesses of her story and Beate herself, she *did* work miracles! Through this event in her life, Beate can become the famous psychoanalyst, who continuously recounts her-stories, laughing at psychoanalysis, marriage, religion, love.

When she is faced with the ghosts of her past, she manages to reverse the situation, and become the hunter instead of being the prey. Although in the beginning she leaves Paris, her job, her lover, and flees to London in order to escape revelation, she finally decides to go back and hunt her hunter with the help of another woman, Lacey Twickenham—another name that alludes to Anna O. again. According to Hunter one of Bertha Pappenheim's lifelong passions was embroidery and lacemaking, an occupation which she associates with the girl's imaginative capacities: "Speculating on the origin of 'hypnoid' (dissociated, split) states, Breuer and Freud note that these conditions often seem to grow out of the daydreams that are common even in healthy people, 'and to which needlework and similar occupations render women especially prone.' That is, people left to embroidery are bound to embroider fantasies" (94). This young woman, Lacey Twickenham, wants to write a book about Lucky Lucan, or rather to write Lucky Lucan in a book, a prospect that he loathes. Thus, she embarks on a manhunt and manages to trace him several times, without however actually pinning him down. When Wolf/Pappenheim finds this accomplice, she regains her power and flies back to Paris to reclaim her position of authority and chase Lucan to Africa, where he is to be killed.

However, it is not only the Pappenheim/Wolf identity that is at stake. The whole novel is preoccupied with the pursuit of identity, involving the readers in this witch-hunt as well. Names are false, identities are assumed, faces are fake, appearances are deceptive. And the reader is called upon to make sense out of non-sense, to add flesh to the skeletons in the closet, or trace the untraceable "stigmata" in this adventurous seduction by the Sparkian (un)reality.

Bibliography

WORKS BY MURIEL SPARK

Note: Abbreviations found in the text appear in parentheses following titles.

The Comforters. (*C*). 1957. Harmondsworth: Penguin, 1963.

Robinson. 1958. Harmondsworth: Penguin, 1964.

"The Portobello Road." (PR). *The Go-Away Bird and Other Stories*. 1958. Harmondsworth: Penguin, 1978. 164–189.

"The Go-Away Bird." (GB). *The Go-Away Bird and Other Stories*. 1958. Harmondsworth: Penguin, 1978. 71–124.

Collected Stories 1. 1958. London: Macmillan, 1985.

Memento Mori. 1959. Harmondsworth: Penguin, 1988.

The Ballad of Peckham Rye. (*BPR*). 1960. Harmondsworth: Penguin, 1984.

The Bachelors. 1960. Harmondsworth: Penguin, 1963.

The Prime of Miss Jean Brodie. (*PMJB*). 1961. Harmondsworth: Penguin, 1983.

"My Conversion." *The Twentieth Century* 170 (Autumn 1961): 58–63.

The Girls of Slender Means. 1963. Harmondsworth: Penguin, 1966.

The Mandelbaum Gate. 1965. London: Macmillan, 1967.

Collected Poems I. London: Macmillan, 1967.

The Public Image. (*PI*). 1968. Harmondsworth: Penguin, 1990.

The Driver's Seat. (*DS*). 1970. Harmondsworth: Penguin, 1988.

Not to Disturb. (*ND*). 1971. Harmondsworth: Penguin, 1974.

The Hothouse by the East River. 1973. London: Macmillan, 1973.

The Abbess of Crewe. 1974. Harmondsworth: Penguin, 1975.

The Takeover. (*T*). 1976. Harmondsworth: Penguin, 1978.

Territorial Rights. 1979. London: Macmillan, 1979.

Loitering with Intent. (*LI*). London: Bodley Head, 1981.

"Bang-bang You're Dead". (BYD). *Bang-bang You're Dead and Other Stories.* London: Granada, 1982.

The Only Problem. (*OP*). London: Bodley Head, 1984.

A Far Cry from Kensington. 1988. Harmondsworth: Penguin, 1989.

Mary Shelley. London: Cardinal, 1989.

Symposium. (*S*). 1990. Harmondsworth: Penguin, 1991.

Curriculum Vitae: Autobiography. (*CV*). London: Constable, 1992.

Reality and Dreams. (*RD*). London: Constable, 1996.

Aiding and Abetting. (*AA*). London: Viking, 2000.

WORKS ABOUT MURIEL SPARK

Bold, Allan, ed. *Muriel Spark: An Odd Capacity for Vision.* London and Totowa: Vision and Barnes and Noble, 1984.

Bradbury, Malcolm. "Muriel Spark's Fingernails." *Possibilities: Essays on the State of the Novel.* London: Oxford University Press, 1973. 247–255.

Dipple, Elizabeth. "Muriel Spark and the Art of the Exclusive." *The Unresolvable Plot: Reading Contemporary Fiction.* London and New York: Routledge, 1988. 140–159.

Edgecombe, Rodney Stenning. *Vocation and Identity in the Fiction of Muriel Spark.* Columbia and London: University of Missouri Press, 1990.

—. *The New Feminist Criticism: Essays on Women, Literature, Theory.* New York: Pantheon Books, 1985.

Frankel, Sara. "An Interview with Muriel Spark." *Partisan Review* 54:3 (1987): 443–457.

Gillham, Ian. "Keeping It Short—Muriel Spark Talks about Her Books to Ian Gillham." *The Listener* 24 Sept. 1970: 41–43.

Green, George. "Du Côté de Chez Disaster: The Novels of Muriel Spark." *Papers on Language and Literature* 16 (Summer 1980): 295–315.

Harrison, Bernard. "Muriel Spark and Jane Austen." *The Modern English Novel: The Reader, The Writer and the Work.* Ed. Gabriel Josipovici. London: Open Books, 1976. 225–251.

Hart, Francis Russell. "Ridiculous Demons." *Muriel Spark: An Odd Capacity for Vision.* Ed. Alan Bold. London and Totowa: Vision and Barnes and Noble, 1984. 23–43.

Hubbard, Tom. "The Liberated Instant: Muriel Spark and the Short Story." In *Muriel Spark: An Odd Capacity for Vision*, ed. Alan Bold. London and Totowa: Vision and Barnes and Noble, 1984. 167–182.

Ivry, Benjamin. "Knowing at Second Hand: Interview with Muriel Spark." *Newsweek* 24 August 1992: 56.

Kane, Richard. *Iris Murdoch, Muriel Spark, and John Fowles: Didactic Demons in Modern Fiction.* London and Toronto: Associated University Presses, 1988.

Kermode, Frank. "Muriel Spark." 1968. *Modern Essays.* Collins: Fontana Books, 1971. 267–283.

—. "The House of Fiction: Interview with Seven English Novelists." *Partisan Review* 21 (1963): 79–82.

Leonard, Joan. "Muriel Spark's Parables: The Religious Limits of Her Art." In *Foundations of Religious Literacy: The Annual Publication of the College Theology Society*, ed. John Apezynski. Chico, California: Scholars Press, 1983. 153–164.

Little, Judy. *Comedy and the Woman Writer: Woolf, Spark and Feminism.* Lincoln: University of Nebraska Press, 1983.

Lodge, David. "The Uses and Abuses of Omniscience: Method and Meaning in Muriel Spark's *The Prime of Miss Jean Brodie*." *The Novelist at the Crossroads and Other Essays on Fiction and Criticism.* London: Routledge and Kegan Paul, 1971. 119–144.

McWilliam, Candia. "Truth's Own Dear Beauty: The Early Years of the Remorseless, Lyrical Mrs Spark." *The Times Literary Supplement* 24 July 1992: 5–6.

Malkoff, Karl. *Muriel Spark.* New York and London: Columbia University Press, 1968.

Massie, Allan. "Calvinism and Catholicism in Muriel Spark." *Muriel Spark: An Odd Capacity for Vision.* Ed. Alan Bold. London and Totowa: Vision and Barnes and Noble, 1984. 94–107.

Mengham, Rod. "1973 The End of History: Cultural Change According to Muriel Spark." *An Introduction to Contemporary Fiction.* Ed. Rod Mengham. Cambridge: Polity Press, 1999. 123–134.

Page, Norman. *Modern Novelists: Muriel Spark.* London: Macmillan Education, 1990.

Parrinder, Patrick. "Muriel Spark and Her Critics." *Critical Quarterly* 25 (summer 1983) : 23–31.

Perrie, Walter. "Mrs. Spark's Verse." *Muriel Spark: An Odd Capacity for Vision.* Ed. Alan Bold. London and Totowa: Vision and Barnes and Noble, 1984. 183–204.

Pullin, Faith. "Autonomy and Fabulation in the Fiction of Muriel Spark." *Muriel Spark: An Odd Capacity for Vision.* Ed. Alan Bold. London and Totowa: Vision and Barnes and Noble, 1984. 70–93.

Randisi, Jennifer L. "Muriel Spark and Satire." *Muriel Spark: An Odd Capacity for Vision*. Ed. Alan Bold. London and Totowa: Vision and Barnes and Noble, 1984. 132–145.

Royle, Trevor. "Spark and Scotland." *Muriel Spark: An Odd Capacity for Vision*. Ed. Alan Bold. London and Totowa: Vision and Barnes and Noble, 1984. 147–166.

Sproxton, Judy. *The Women of Muriel Spark*. London: Constable, 1992.

Toynbee, Philip. "Interview with Muriel Spark." *The Observer* 7 November 1971: 73–74.

Whittaker, Ruth. *The Faith and Fiction of Muriel Spark*. London: The Macmillan Press, 1982.

GENERAL THEORETICAL TEXTS

Abraham, Nicolas, and Maria Torok. *The Wolf Man's Magic Word*. Trans. Nicolas Rand. Minneapolis: University of Minnesota Press, 1986.

Alliez, Eric, and Michel Feher. "Reflections of a Soul." *Fragments for a History of the Human Body, Part II*. Ed. Michel Feher. New York: Zone, 1989. 46–85.

Althusser, Louis. *Essays on Ideology*. London: Verso, 1984.

Anglo, Sydney, ed. *The Damned Art: Essays in the Literature of Witchcraft*. London, Henley and Boston: Routledge and Kegan Paul, 1977.

—. "Evident Authority and Authoritative Evidence: The *Maleus Maleficarum*." Ed. Anglo Sydney. *The Damned Art: Essays in the Literature of Witchcraft*. London, Henley and Boston: Routledge and Kegan Paul, 1977. 1–31.

Ariès, Philippe. *The Hour of Our Death*. 1983. Trans. Helen Weaver. Harmondsworth: Penguin, 1987.

Aristotle. "Poetics." *Aristotle's Poetics, Demetrius on Style, Longinus on the Sublime*. Trans. John Warrington. London: Dent and Sons, 1963. 3–60.

Armstrong, Karen. *A History of God. From Abraham to the Present: The 4000-year Quest for God*. London: Mandarin, 1994.

Bachelard, Gaston. *The Right to Dream*. Trans. J. A. Underwood. Dallas: The Dallas Institute Publications, 1988.

—. "Shells." *The Poetics of Space*. Trans. Maria Jolas. Boston: Beacon Press, 1969. 105–135.

Bal, Mieke. "The Rape of Narrative and the Narrative of Rape: Speech Acts and Body Language in Judges." *Literature and the Body: Essays on Populations and Persons*. Ed. Elaine Scarry. Baltimore: The Johns Hopkins University Press, 1988. 1–32.

Balibar, Etienne, and Pierre Macherey. "On Literature as an Ideological Form." Trans. Ian McLeod, John Whitehead and Ann Wordsworth. *Untying the Text: A Post-Structuralist Reader*. Ed. Robert Young. Boston, London, and Henley: Routledge and Kegan Paul. 1981. 79–99.

Barker, Francis. "A Challenged Spectacle." *The Tremulous Private Body: Essays on Subjection.* New York and London: Methuen, 1984.

Barthes, Roland. *A Lover's Discourse: Fragments.* Trans. Richard Howard. New York: Hill and Wang, 1978.

—. *Camera Lucida: Reflections on Photography.* Trans. Richard Howard. London: Jonathan Cape, 1982.

—. *Critical Essays.* Trans. Richard Howard. New York: Northwestern University Press, 1972.

—. "From Work to Text." *Image Music Text.* 1977. Trans. Stephen Heath. New York: Fontana, 1982. 155–164.

—. *Mythologies.* 1973. Trans. Annette Lavers. London: Paladin, 1984.

—. "Rhetoric of the Image." *Image Music Text.* 1977. Trans. Stephen Heath. New York: Fontana, 1982. 32–51.

—. *Roland Barthes by Roland Barthes.* Trans. Richard Howard. New York: Hill and Wang, 1977.

—. *S/Z: An Essay.* Trans. Richard Miller. New York: Hill and Wang, 1974.

—. "The Death of the Author." *Image Music Text.* 1977. Trans. Stephen Heath. New York: Fontana, 1982. 142–148.

—. "Theory of the Text." 1973. Trans. Ian McLeod. *Untying the Text: A Post-Structuralist Reader.* Ed. Robert Young. Boston, London, and Henley: Routledge and Kegan Paul. 1981. 31–47.

—. *The Pleasure of the Text.* Trans. Richard Miller. New York: Hill and Wang, 1975.

—. "The Photographic Message." *Image Music Text.* 1977. Trans. Stephen Heath. New York: Fontana, 1982. 15–31.

—. *The Responsibility of Forms: Critical Essays on Music, Art, and Representation.* Trans. Richard Howard. New York: Hill and Wang, 1986.

Baudrillard, Jean. *Cool Memories.* Trans. Chris Turner. London and New York: Verso, 1990.

—. *Fatal Strategies.* Ed. Jim Fleming. Trans. Philip Beitchman and W. G. J. Niesluchowski. New York and London: Semiotext(e) and Pluto, 1990.

—. *Forget Foucault.* New York: Semiotext(e), 1987.

—. *In the Shadow of the Silent Majorities.* Trans. Paul Foss, John Johnston, and Paul Patton. New York: Semiotext(e), 1983.

—. *Jean Baudrillard: Selected Writings.* 1988. Ed. Mark Poster. Cambridge: Polity Press, 1992.

—. "On Seduction." *Jean Baudrillard: Selected Writings.* 1988. Ed. Mark Poster. Cambridge: Polity Press, 1992.

—. *Seduction.* 1979. Trans. Brian Singer. New York: St. Martin's Press, 1990.

—. *Simulations.* Trans. Paul Foss, Paul Patton, and Philip Beitchman. New York: Semiotext(e), 1983.

—. *Symbolic Exchange and Death.* Trans. Iain Hamilton Grant. London: Sage Publications, 1993.

—. *The Ecstasy of Communication.* Ed. Sylvére Lotringer. Trans. Bernard and Caroline Schutze. New York: Semiotext(e), 1988.

—. *The Transparency of Evil: Essays on Extreme Phenomena.* Trans. James Benedict. London and New York: Verso, 1993.

Baxter, Christopher. "Johann Weyer's *De Praestigiis Daemonum*: Unsystematic Psychopathology." Ed. Anglo Sydney. *The Damned Art: Essays in the Literature of Witchcraft.* London, Henley and Boston: Routledge and Kegan Paul, 1977. 53–75.

—. "Jean Bodin's *De la Démonomanie des Sorciers*: The Logic of Persecution." Ed. Anglo Sydney. *The Damned Art: Essays in the Literature of Witchcraft.* London, Henley and Boston: Routledge and Kegan Paul, 1977. 76–105

Benjamin, Jessica. "Master and Slave." *The Bonds of Love: Psychoanalysis, Feminism, and the Problem of Domination.* New York: Pantheon Books, 1988. 51–84.

Benjamin, Walter. "The Work of Art in the Age of Mechanical Reproduction." *Illuminations.* Ed. Hannah Arendt. Trans. Harry Zohn. London: Jonathan Cape, 1970.

Benvenutto, B., and R. Kennedy. *The Works of Jacques Lacan: An Introduction.* London: Free Association Books, 1986.

Berger, John. *Ways of Seeing.* 1972. Harmondsworth: British Broadcasting Corporation and Penguin Books, 1984.

Bernstein, Susan David. "Confessing Lacan." *Seduction and Theory: Readings of Gender, Representation, and Rhetoric.* Ed. Dianne Hunter. Urbana and Chicago: University of Illinois Press, 1989. 195–213.

Bertens, Hans. "The Postmodern *Weltanschauung* and its Relations with Postmodernism: An Introductory Survey." *Approaching Postmodernism: Papers Presented at a Workshop on Postmodernism, 21–23 September 1984, University of Utrecht.* Eds. Douwe Fokkema and Hans Bertens. Amsterdam and Philadelphia: John Benjamin's Publishing Company, 1986. 9–51.

Black, Elizabeth. "The Nature of Fictional Discourse: A Case Study." *Applied Linguistics* 10: 3 (September 1989): 281–293.

Blanchot, Maurice. "Michel Foucault as I Imagine Him." 1986. *Foucault / Blanchot.* Trans. Jeffrey Mehlman and Brian Massumi. New York: Zone Books, 1987. 61–109.

—. *The Sirens' Song: Selected Essays by Maurice Blanchot.* Ed. Gabriel Josipovici. Trans. Sacha Rabinovitch. Sussex: The Harvester Press, 1982.

—. *The Space of Literature*. 1955. Trans. Ann Smock. Lincoln and London: University of Nebraska Press, 1992.

—. *The Writing of the Disaster*. Trans. Ann Smock. Lincoln and London: University of Nebraska Press, 1986.

Bouchard, Larry. *Tragic Method and Tragic Theology: Evil in Contemporary Drama and Religious Thought*. University Park and London: The Pennsylvania State University Press, 1989.

Brant, Clare. "Speaking of Women: Scandal and the Law in the Mid-Eighteenth Century." *Women, Texts and Histories 1570–1760*. Eds. Clare Brant and Diane Purkiss. London and New York: Routledge, 1992. 242–270.

Brennan, Teresa. "Introduction." *Between Feminism and Psychoanalysis*. Ed. Teresa Brenan. London and New York: Routledge, 1989. 1–23.

Bronfen, Elisabeth. *Over Her Dead Body. Death, Femininity and the Aesthetic*. Manchester: Manchester University Press, 1992.

Brooke-Rose, Christine. "The Dissolution of Character in the Novel." *Reconstructing Individualism: Autonomy, Individuality and the Self in Western Thought*. Eds. Thomas Heller, Morton Sosna and David Wellbery. Stanford, California: Stanford University Press, 1986. 184–196.

Brooks, Peter. *Body Work: Objects of Desire in Modern Narrative*. Cambridge and London: Harvard University Press, 1993.

—. *Reading for the Plot: Design and Intention in Narrative*. Oxford: Clarendon Press, 1984.

Burke, Peter. "Witchcraft and Magic in Renaissance Italy: Gianfrancesco Pico and his *Strix*." Ed. Anglo Sydney. *The Damned Art: Essays in the Literature of Witchcraft*. London, Henley, and Boston: Routledge and Kegan Paul, 1977. 32–52.

Burkert, Walter. *Homo Necans. The Anthropology of Ancient Greek Sacrificial Ritual*. 1972. Trans. Peter Bing. California: University of California Press, 1983.

Cahoone, Lawrence, ed. "Introduction." *From Modernism to Post-modernism: An Anthology*. Cambridge, Massachusetts: Blackwell, 1996. 1–23.

Calinescu, Matei. "Postmodernism and Some Paradoxes of Periodization." and "The Presence of Postmodernism in British Fiction: Aspects of Style and Selfhood." *Approaching Postmodernism: Papers Presented at a Workshop on Postmodernism, 21–23 September 1984, University of Utrecht*. Eds. Douwe Fokkema and Hans Bertens. Amsterdam and Philadelphia: John Benjamin's Publishing Company, 1986. 239–254.

Cantarella, Eva. "Dangling Virgins: Myth, Ritual, and the Place of Women in Ancient Greece." *The Female Body in Western Culture*. Ed. Susan Rubin Suleiman. Cambridge: Harvard University Press, 1986.

Carmichael, Thomas. "Postmodernism, Symbolicity, and the Rhetoric of the Hyperreal: Kenneth Burke, Fredric Jameson, and Jean Baudrillard." *Text and Performance Quarterly* 11 (1991): 319–324.

Carroll, David. *The Subject in Question: The Languages of Theory and the Strategies of Fiction.* Chicago and London: The University of Chicago Press, 1982.

Carter, Angela. *The Sadeian Woman: An Exercise in Cultural History.* 1979. London: Virago Press, 1992.

Cellini, Benvenuto. *Autobiography.* Trans. George Bull. Harmondsworth: Penguin, 1956.

Chambers, Ross. *Story and Situation: Narrative Seduction and the Power of Fiction.* Minneapolis: University of Minnesota Press, 1984.

Chase, Cynthia. "'Transference' as Trope and Persuasion." *Discourse in Psychoanalysis and Literature.* Ed. Shlomith Rimmon-Kenan. London and New York: Methuen, 1987. 211–232.

Chatman, Seymour. *Story and Discourse: Narrative Structure in Fiction and Film.* Ithaca and London: Cornell University Press, 1978.

Chesler, Phyllis. *Women and Madness.* New York: Avon Books, 1972.

Cixous, Hélène. "Castration or Decapitation." Trans. Annette Kuhn. *Contemporary Literary Criticism: Literary and Cultural Studies.* Ed. Robert Con Davis and Ronald Schleifer. New York: Longman, 1989. 479–491.

—. "The Laugh of the Medusa." *New French Feminisms: An Anthology.* Eds. Elaine Marks and Isabelle de Courtivron. Sussex: The Harvester Press, 1981. 245–64.

Cixous, Hélène, and Catherine Clément. "Seduction and Guilt." The *Newly Born Woman.* Trans. Betsy Wing. Minneapolis and London: University of Minnesota Press, 1986. 40–57.

Coates, Paul. "Franz Kafka: The Impossibility of Writing." *The Realist Fantasy. Fiction and Reality Since* Clarissa. London: The Macmillan Press, 1983. 158–179.

Connor, Steven. *Postmodernist Culture: An Introduction to Theories of the Contemporary.* 1989. Oxford: Basil Blackwell, 1990.

Copjec, Joan. "Cutting up." *Between Feminism and Psychoanalysis.* Ed. Teresa Brenan. London and New York: Routledge, 1989. 227–246.

Culler, Jonathan. "Introduction." *On Deconstruction: Theory and Criticism after Structuralism.* London, Melbourne, and Henley: Routledge and Kegan Paul, 1983.

—. *Structuralist Poetics: Structuralism, Linguistics and the Study of Literature.* London: Routledge and Kegan Paul, 1975.

Dällenbach, Lucien. *The Mirror in the Text.* Trans. Jeremy Whiteley and Emma Hughes. Cambridge: Polity Press, 1989.

Davis, Robert Con. "Critical Introduction: The Discourse of the Father" and "Epilogue: The Discourse of Jacques Lacan." *The Fictional Father: Lacanian Readings of the*

Text. Ed. Robert Con Davis. Amherst: The University of Massachusetts Press, 1981. 1–26, 183–189.

Davis, Robert Con, and Ronald Schleifer. *Contemporary Literary Criticism: Literary and Cultural Studies.* New York and London: Longman, 1989.

Debord, Guy. *Society of Spectacle.* 1967. Detroit: Black and Red, 1983.

De Lauretis, Teresa. "Aesthetic and Feminist Theory: Rethinking Women's Cinema." *New German Critique* 34 (winter 1985): 154–175.

Derrida, Jacques. *Writing and Difference.* Trans. Alan Bass. Chicago: The University of Chicago Press, 1987.

—. "Structure, Sign, and Play in the Discourse of the Human Sciences." Trans. Richard Macksey. *Contemporary Literary Criticism: Literary and Cultural Studies.* Ed. Robert Con Davis and Ronald Schleifer. New York: Longman, 1989. 229–248.

—. "The End of the Book and the Beginning of Writing." *From Modernism to Postmodernism: An Anthology.* Ed. Lawrence Cahoone. Cambridge, Massachusetts: Blackwell, 1996. 336–359.

Dijkstra, Bram. "Gynanders and Genetics: Connoisseurs of Bestiality and Serpentine Delights: Leda, Circe, and the Cold Caresses of the Sphinx." *Idols of Perversity. Fantasies of Feminine Evil in Fin-de-Siécle Culture.* New York and Oxford: Oxford University Press, 1986. 272–332.

Doanne, Mary Ann. *The Desire to Desire: The Woman's Film of the 1940s.* Bloomington and Indianapolis: Indiana University Press, 1987.

Docherty, Thomas, ed. *Postmodernism: A Reader.* Hempstead: Harvester Wheatsheaf, 1993.

—. "Postmodernism: An Introduction." Ed. Thomas Docherty. *Postmodernism: A Reader.* Hempstead: Harvester Wheatsheaf, 1993. 1–31.

Donne, Williams Bodhum. "The Two Iphigenias." *Euripides.* Edinburgh: William Blackwood and Sons. 100–121.

Dowen, Ken. *Death and the Maiden: Girl's Initiation Rites in Greek Mythology.* London and New York: Routledge, 1989.

DuBois, Page. *Sowing the Body: Psychoanalysis and Ancient Representations of Women.* Chicago: The University of Chicago Press, 1988.

Eagleton, Terry. *Literary Theory: An Introduction.* 1983. Oxford: Basil Blackwell, 1988.

—. *Marxism and Literary Criticism.* California: University of California Press, 1976.

Easlea, Brian. *Witch-hunting, Magic and the New Philosophy: An Introduction to Debates of the Scientific Revolution 1450–1750.* New York and London: Harvester Wheatsheaf, 1980.

Eliade, Mircea. *Gods, Goddesses, and Myths of Creation: A Thematic Source Book of the History of Religions.* 1967. New York: Harper and Row, 1974.

—. *Myths, Rites, Symbols,* Vol. 2. Ed. Wendell Beane and William Doty. New York: Harper and Row Publishers, 1976.

—. *Occultism, Witchcraft, and Cultural Fashions: Essays in Comparative Religions.* Chicago and London: Chicago University Press, 1976.

—. *The Two and the One.* 1962. Trans. J. M. Cohen. Chicago: The University of Chicago Press, 1982.

Evans, Martha Noel. "Hysteria and the Seduction of Theory." *Seduction and Theory: Readings of Gender, Representation and Rhetoric.* Ed. Dianne Hunter. Urbana and Chicago: University of Illinois Press, 1989. 73–85.

Felman, Shoshana. "Beyond Oedipus: The Specimen Story of Psycho-analysis." *Lacan and Narration: The Psychoanalytic Difference in Narrative Theory.* 1983. Ed. Robert Con Davis. Baltimore and London: The Johns Hopkins University Press, 1985. 1021–1053.

Ferguson, George. *Signs and Symbols in Christian Art.* 1961. New York: Oxford University Press, 1989.

Ferguson, John. *Among the Gods: An Archaeological Exploration of Ancient Greek Religion.* London and New York: Routledge, 1989.

Fokkema, Douwe, and Hans Bertens, eds. *Approaching Postmodernism: Papers Presented at a Workshop on Postmodernism, 21–23 September 1984, University of Utrecht.* Amsterdam and Philadelphia: John Benjamin's Publishing Company, 1986.

Forrester, John. "The True Story of Anna O." *The Seduction of Psychoanalysis: Freud, Lacan and Derrida.* Cambridge: Cambridge University Press, 1990.

Foucault, Michel. "Language to Infinity." *Michel Foucault: Language, Counter-Memory, Practice. Selected Essays and Interviews.* Ed. Donald F. Bouchard. Trans. Donald F. Bouchard and Sherry Simon. Oxford: Basil Blackwell, 1977. 53–67.

—. *Madness and Civilization: A History of Insanity in the Age of Reason.* Trans. Richard Howard. New York: Vintage Books, 1988.

—. "Maurice Blanchot: The Thought from Outside." 1986. *Foucault / Blanchot.* Trans. Jeffrey Mehlman and Brian Massumi. New York: Zone Books, 1987. 8–58.

—. *The History of Sexuality.* Vol. 1: *An Introduction.* Trans. Robert Hurly. Harmondsworth: Penguin, 1984.

—. "The Order of Discourse." 1970. Trans. Ian McLeod. *Untying the Text: A Post-Structuralist Reader.* Ed. Robert Young. Boston, London, and Henley: Routledge and Kegan Paul. 1981. 48–78.

—. *The Order of Things: An Archaeology of the Human Sciences.* New York: Pantheon Books, 1971.

—. "The Subject and Power." *Michel Foucault: Beyond Structuralism and Hermeneutics.* Eds. Hubert Dreyfus and Paul Rabinow. Brighton: Harvester, 1982. 208–226.

—. "What is an Author?" *Textual Strategies: Perspectives in Post-Structuralist Criticism.* Ed. Josué V. Harari. Ithaca, New York: Cornell University Press, 1979. 141–160.

Frazer, Sir James George. *The Golden Bough: A Study in Magic and Religion.* 1922. London: Papermac, 1992.

Freccero, John. "Autobiography and Narrative." *Reconstructing Individualism: Autonomy, Individuality and the Self in Western Thought.* Eds. Thomas Heller, Morton Sosna and David Wellbery. Stanford, California: Stanford University Press, 1986. 16–29.

Freud, Sigmund. *Civilization and its Discontents. Civilization, Society and Religion: Group Psychology and Its Discontents and Other Works.* 1985. Trans. James Strachey. Harmondsworth: Penguin, 1987. 243–340.

—. *On Metapsychology: The Theory of Psychoanalysis/ Beyond the Pleasure Principle the Ego the Id and Other Works.* Trans. James Strachey. Harmondsworth: Penguin, 1985.

—. *On Sexuality: Three Essays on the Theory of Sexuality and Other Works.* Trans. James Strachey. Harmondsworth: Penguin, 1991.

—. *The Origins of Religion: Totem and Taboo, Moses and Monotheism and Other Works.* Trans. James Strachey. Harmondsworth: Penguin, 1985.

—. "The Theme of the Tree Caskets." *Art and Literature. Jensen's* Gradiva, *Leonardo Da Vinci and Other Works.* 1985. Ed. Albert Dickson. Trans. James Strachey. Harmondsworth: Penguin, 1987. 233–247.

—. "The Uncanny." 1919. *Art and Literature. Jensen's* Gradiva, *Leonardo Da Vinci and Other Works.* 1985. Ed. Albert Dickson. Trans. James Strachey. Harmondsworth: Penguin, 1987. 335–376.

—. "Thoughts for the Times on War and Death." *Civilization, Society and Religion: Group Psychology and Its Discontents and Other Works.* 1985. Trans. James Strachey. Harmondsworth: Penguin, 1987. 57–90.

Freud, Sigmund, and Joseph Breuer. *Studies on Hysteria.* 1974. Trans. James and Alix Strachey. Harmondsworth: Penguin, 1986.

Fromm, Erich. "Franz Kafka." *Literature and Psychoanalysis.* Eds. Edith Kurzwei and William Phillips. New York: Columbia University Press, 1983. 261–269.

Frow, John. "Intertextuality and Ontology." *Intertextuality: Theories and Practices.* Eds. Michael Worton and Judith Still. Manchester and New York: Manchester University Press, 1990. 45–55.

Frye, Northrop. *The Double Vision: Language and Meaning in Religion.* Toronto: The University of Toronto Press, 1991.

Gallop, Jane. *The Daughter's Seduction. Feminism and Psychoanalysis.* 1982. New York: Cornell University Press, 1983.

—. *Thinking Through the Body.* New York: Columbia University Press, 1988.

Gamman, Lorraine, and Margaret Marshment, eds. *The Female Gaze: Women as Viewers of Popular Culture*. London: The Women's Press, 1988.

Gelpi, Albert. "Emily Dickinson and the Deerslayer: The Dilemma of the Woman Poet in America." *Shakespeare's Sisters. Feminist Essays on Women Poets*. Eds. Sandra Gilbert and Susan Gubar. Bloomington: Indiana University Press, 1979. 122–134.

Genette, Gérard. *Narrative Discourse: An Essay in Method*. Trans. Jane E. Lewin. Ithaca, New York: Cornell University Press, 1980.

—. "Proust Palimpsest." 1961. *Figures of Literary Discourse*. Trans. Alan Sheridan. Oxford: Basil Blackwell, 1982. 203–228.

—. "The Obverse of Signs." 1964. *Figures of Literary Discourse*. Trans. Alan Sheridan. Oxford: Basil Blackwell, 1982. 27–44.

Gilbert, Sandra, and Susan Gubar. "Toward a Feminist Poetics." *The Madwoman in the Attic. The Woman Writer and the Nineteenth-Century Imagination*. 1979. New Haven: Yale University Press, 1984. 1–104.

Gombrich, E. H. "A Crisis of Art." *The Story of Art*. 1950. Oxford: Phaidon Press, 1991. 277–300.

—. "Freud's Aesthetics." *Meditations on the History of Art*. Ed. Richard Woodfierd. Oxford: Phaidon Press, 1987. 221–239.

Graves, Robert. *The Greek Myths*. Vol. 1. Harmondsworth: Penguin, 1955.

Gregg, John. "Blanchot's Suicidal Artist: Writing and the (Im)Possibility of Death." *Substance: A Review of Theory and Literary Criticism* 17:1 (1988): 47–58.

Grigg, Russell. "Signifier, Object, and the Transference." *Lacan and the Subject of Language*. Eds. Ellie Ragland-Sullivan and Mark Bracher. New York and London: Routledge, 1991. 100–115.

Grosz, Elizabeth. *Jacques Lacan: A Feminist Introduction*. London and New York: Routledge, 1990.

Gubar, Susan. "Representing Pornography: Feminism, Criticism, and Depictions of Female Violation." *Critical Inquiry* 13:4 (summer 1987): 712–741.

—. "'The Blank Page' and the Issues of Female Creativity." *Critical Inquiry* 8 (winter 1981): 243–263.

Gurevitch, Michael et al., eds. *Culture, Society and the Media*. London and New York: Routledge, 1992.

Habermas, Jürgen. "The Entry into Postmodernity: Nietzsche as a Turning Point" and "Modernity—An Incomplete Project." *Postmodernism: A Reader*. Ed. Thomas Docherty. Hempstead: Harvester Wheatsheaf, 1993. 51–61, 98–109.

Hamilton, Edith. *Mythology. Timeless Tales of Gods and Heroes*. New York: Mentor Books, 1942.

Hassan, Ihab. "POSTmodernISM: A Paracritical Bibliography." 1975. *From Modernism to Post-modernism: An Anthology.* Ed. Lawrence Cahoone. Cambridge, Massachusetts: Blackwell, 1996. 382–400.

Hayman, Ronald. "Kafka and the Mice." *Literature and Psychoanalysis.* Eds. Edith Kurzwei and William Phillips. New York: Columbia University Press, 1983. 290–299.

Heath, Steven. "Joan Riviere and the Masquerade." *Formations of Fantasy.* Eds. Victor Burgin et al. London: Routledge, 1986. 45–61.

Heckman, Susan. *Gender and Knowledge: Elements of a Postmodern Feminism.* Boston: Northeastern University Press, 1992.

Heller, Thomas, Morton Sosna, and David Wellbery, eds. *Reconstructing Individualism: Autonomy, Individuality and the Self in Western Thought.* Stanford, California: Stanford University Press, 1986. 16–29.

Hester, Marianne. *Lewd Women and Wicked Witches. A Study of the Dynamics of Male Dominance.* London and New York: Routledge, 1992.

Higonnet, Margaret. "Speaking Silences: Women's Suicide." *The Female Body in Western Culture.* Ed. Susan Rubin Suleiman. Cambridge: Harvard University Press, 1986. 68–83.

Hill, Christopher. *Antichrist in Seventeenth Century England.* London and New York: Verso, 1990.

Horkheimer, Max, and Theodor W. Adorno. 1944. *Dialectic of Enlightenment.* Trans. John Cumming. New York: Continuum, 1989.

Hunter, Dianne. "Hysteria, Psychoanalysis, and Feminism: The Case of Anna O." 1983. *The (M)other Tongue: Essays in Psychoanalytic Interpretation.* Eds. Shirley Nelson Garner, Claire Kahane, and Madelon Sprengnether. Ithaca and London: Cornell University Press, 1985.

—. "Introduction." *Seduction and Theory: Readings of Gender, Representation, and Rhetoric.* Ed. Dianne Hunter. Urbana and Chicago: University of Illinois Press, 1989. 1–10.

Hutcheon, Linda. *Narcissistic Narrative. The Metaphysical Paradox.* 1980. New York and London: Methuen, 1984.

—. *The Politics of Postmodernism.* 1989. London and New York: Routledge, 1990.

Huyssen, Andreas. "Mapping the Postmodern." *After the Great Divide: Modernism, Mass Culture, Postmodernism.* Bloomington and Indianapolis: Indiana University Press, 1986. 178–221.

Irigaray, Luce. *Marine Lover of Friedrich Nietzsche.* Trans. Gillian Gill. New York: Columbia University Press, 1991.

—. *Speculum of the Other Woman.* 1974. Trans. Gillian Gill. Ithaca: Cornell University Press, 1985.

—. *This Sex Which Is Not One*. Trans. Catherine Porter. Ithaca: Cornell University Press, 1985.

Jameson, Fredric. "Imaginary and Symbolic in Lacan: Marxism, Psychoanalytic Criticism and the Problem of the Subject." *Literature and Psychoanalysis: The Question of Reading: Otherwise*. 1977. Ed. Shoshana Felman. Baltimore and London: The Johns Hopkins University Press, 1982. 338–395.

—. "Reification and Utopia in Mass Culture." 1979. *Signatures of the Visible*. New York and London: Routledge, 1990.

Jasipovici, Gabriel. "The World and the Book." *The World and the Book. A Study in Modern Fiction*. Stanford: Stanford University Press, 1971. 286–309.

Jenny, Laurent. "The Strategy of Form." *French Literary Theory: A Reader*. Ed. Tzvetan Todorov. Trans. R. Carter. Cambridge and Paris: Cambridge University Press and Editions de la Maison des Sciences de l'Homme, 1982. 34–63.

Kaplan, Ann. *Women and Film: Both Sides of the Cinema*. London and New York: Routledge, 1983.

Kappeler, Susanne. *The Pornography of Representation*. Cambridge: Polity Press, 1986.

Kaufmann, Walter, ed. *Existentialism, Religion, and Death: Thirteen Essays*. New York: New American Library, 1976.

Kearney, Richard. *Poetics of Imagining: From Husserl to Lyotard. (Problems of Modern European Thought)* London: HarperCollins Academic, 1991.

Kellner, Douglas. *Jean Baudrillard: From Marxism to Postmodernism and Beyond*. Stanford, California: Stanford University Press, 1989.

Kermode, Frank. *The Sense of an Ending: Studies in the Theory of Fiction*. 1968. Oxford: Oxford University Press, 1975.

Kierkegaard, S. *Gospel of Sufferings*. Trans. A. S. Aldworth and W. S. Ferrie. London: The Camelot Press, 1955.

Kofman, Sarah. *The Enigma of Woman: Women in Freud's Writing*. Trans. Catherine Porter. Ithaca: Cornell University Press, 1988.

Kristeva, Julia. *Black Sun: Depression and Melancholia*. Trans. Leon Roudiez. New York: Columbia University Press, 1989.

—. *Desire in Language: A Semiotic Approach to Literature and Art*. 1981. Ed. Leon S. Roudiez. Trans. Thomas Gora, Alice Jardine, and Leon S. Roudiez. Oxford: Basil Blackwell, 1989.

—. "On the Melancholic Imaginary." Trans. Louise Burchill. *Discourse in Psychoanalysis and Literature*. Ed. Sholith Rimmon-Kenan. London and New York: Methuen, 1987. 104–123.

—. *Powers of Horror. An Essay on Abjection*. Trans. Leon Roudiez. New York: Columbia University Press, 1982.

—. *Tales of Love*. 1983. Trans. Leon Roudiez. New York: Columbia University Press, 1987.

Kutzman, Lawrence D., ed. *Michel Foucault: Politics, Philosophy, Culture. Interviews and Other Writings: 1977–1984*. Trans. Alan Sheridan and Others. New York and London: Routledge, 1990.

Lacan, Jacques. "The Agency of the Letter in the Unconscious or Reason since Freud." *Écrits: A Selection*. 1977. Trans. Alan Sheridan. London: Tavistock Publications, 1993. 146–178.

—. "Of the Gaze as *Objet Petit a.*" *The Four Fundamental Concepts of Psychoanalysis*. Trans. Alan Sheridan. Ed. Jacques-Alain Miller. Harmondsworth: Penguin, 1979. 67–119.

—. "The Function and Field of Speech and Language in Psychoanalysis." *Écrits: A Selection*. 1977. Trans. Alan Sheridan. London: Tavistock Publications, 1993. 30–113.

—. "The Mirror Stage as Formative of the Function of the I." *Écrits: A Selection*. 1977. Trans. Alan Sheridan. London and New York: Routledge, 1993. 1–7.

—. "The Signification of the Phallus." *Écrits: A Selection*. 1977. Trans. Alan Sheridan. London and New York: Routledge, 1993. 281–291.

—. "The Subversion of the Subject and the Dialectic of Desire in the Freudian Unconscious." *Écrits: A Selection*. 1977. Trans. Alan Sheridan. London and New York: Routledge, 1993. 292–325.

Lane, Jeremy. "His Master's Voice? The Questioning of Authority in Literature." *The Modern English Novel: The Reader, The Writer and the Work*. Ed. Gabriel Josipovici. London: Open Books, 1976. 113–129.

Lanhers, Yvonne. "Joan of Arc, Saint." *Encyclopedia Britanica. Macropaedia*. 1973–1974 ed.

Laplanche, Jean. *Life and Death in Psychoanalysis*. 1985. Trans. Jeffrey Mehlman. Baltimore and London: The Johns Hopkins University Press, 1990.

Larner, Christina. *Witchcraft and Religion: The Politics of Popular Belief*. Oxford and New York: Basil Blackwell, 1984.

—. "The Later Scottish Witchcraft Tracts: *Witch-craft Proven* and *The Tryal of Witchcraft*." Ed. Anglo Sydney. *The Damned Art: Essays in the Literature of Witchcraft*. London, Henley, and Boston: Routledge and Kegan Paul, 1977. 227–245.

Lejeune, Philippe. "The Autobiographical Contract." *French Literary Theory: A Reader*. Ed. Tzvetan Todorov. Trans. R. Carter. Cambridge and Paris: Cambridge University Press and Editions de la Maison des Sciences de l'Homme, 1982. 192–222.

Lemaire, Anika. "Philosophy of Language in Jacques Lacan." *Jacques Lacan*. 1977. Trans. David Masey. London, Boston, and Henley: Routledge and Kegan Paul, 1981.

—. "The Role of the Oedipus in Accession to the Symbolic." *Jacques Lacan*. 1977. Trans. David Masey. London, Boston, and Henley: Routledge and Kegan Paul, 1981.

Luccioni, Eugénie Lemoine. *The Dividing of Women or Woman's Lot*. Trans. Marie-Laure Davenport and Marie-Christine Réguis. London: Free Association Books, 1987.

Lyotard, Jean-François. "Answering the Question: What is Postmodernism?" and "Note on the Meaning of 'Post-'." Ed. Thomas Docherty. *Postmodernism: A Reader*. Hempstead: Harvester Wheatsheaf, 1993. 38–50.

—. *The Postmodern Condition: A Report on Knowledge*. Trans. Geoff Bennington, and Brian Massumi. Minneapolis: University of Minnesota Press, 1984.

McCannell, Juliet Flower. "Oedipus Wrecks: Lacan, Stendhal and the Narrative Form of the Real." *Lacan and Narration: The Psychoanalytic Difference in Narrative Theory*. 1983. Ed. Robert Con Davis. Baltimore and London: The Johns Hopkins University Press, 1985. 910–940.

McCoy, Marjorie Casebier. *To Die With Style*. New York: Abdington Press, 1974.

McDermott, Emily. "Kai ta dokethent' ouk etelesthe." *Euripides'* Medea. *The Incarnation of Disorder*. Pennsylvania: The Pennsylvania State University Press, 1989. 65–80.

McHale, Brian. *Postmodern Fiction*. New York and London: Methuen, 1987.

—. "Change of Dominant from Modernist to Postmodernist Writing." *Approaching Postmodernism: Papers Presented at a Workshop on Postmodernism, 21–23 September 1984, University of Utrecht*. Eds. Douwe Fokkema and Hans Bertens. Amsterdam and Philadelphia: John Benjamin's Publishing Company, 1986. 53–79.

Macherey, Pierre. "The Text Says What it Does Not Say." Trans. G. Wall. 1966. *Literature in the Modern World: Critical Essays and Documents*. Ed. Dennis Walder. Oxford: Oxford University Press, 1990. 215–222.

Marcus, Laura. *Auto/biographical Discourse: Theory, Criticism, Practice*. Manchester and New York: Manchester University Press, 1994.

Marcus, Steven. "Freud and Dora: Story, History, Case History." *Literature and Psychoanalysis*. Ed. Edith Kurzweill and William Phillips. New York: Columbia University Press, 1983.

Marcuse, Herbert. *Eros and Civilization: A Philosophical Inquiry into Freud*. New York: Vintage Books, 1955.

Marks, Elaine, and Isabelle de Courtivron. *New French Feminisms: An Anthology*. Sussex: The Harvester Press, 1981.

Marshall, Brenda K. *Teaching the Postmodern: Fiction and Theory*. New York and London: Routledge, 1992.

Martin, Philip. *Mad Women in Romantic Writing*. Sussex: The Harvester Press, 1987.

Mascetti, Manuela Dunn. *The Song of Eve: Mythology and Symbols of the Goddess*. New York: Simon and Schuster, 1990.

Mayne, Judith. "Spectacle and Narrative." *The Woman at the Keyhole: Feminism and Women's Cinema*. Bloomington: Indiana University Press, 1990. 11–86.

Meaney, Gerardine. *(Un)Like Subjects: Women, Theory, Fiction*. London and New York: Routledge, 1993.

Metzger, Arnold. *Freedom and Death*. Trans. Ralph Manheim. London: Human Context Books, 1973.

Miller, Hillis. "The Figure in the Carpet." 1980. *Modern Literary Theory: A Reader*. London: Edward Arnold Press, 1993. 172–185.

Miller, Jacques-Alain. "Language: Much Ado About What?" *Lacan and the Subject of Language*. Eds. Ellie Ragland-Sullivan and Marc Bracher. New York and London: Routledge, 1991. 21–35.

Miller, Jacques-Alain. "Language: Much Ado About What?." *Lacan and the Subject of Language*. Eds. Ellie Ragland-Sullivan and Mark Bracher. New York and London: Routledge, 1991. 21–35.

Millett, Kate. *Sexual Politics*. London: Virago Press, 1977.

Mitchell, Juliet. *Women: The Longest Revolution. Essays on Feminism, Literature and Psychoanalysis*. London: Virago Press, 1984.

Moers, Ellen. "Female Gothic." *Literary Women*. 1977. London: The Women's Press, 1978. 90–110.

Moi, Toril. *Sexual/Textual Politics: Feminist Literary Theory*. New York and London: Methuen, 1985.

Moran, Richard. "Seeing and Believing: Metaphor, Image, and Force." *Critical Inquiry* 16:1 (autumn 1989): 87–112

Mulvey, Laura. "Visual Pleasure and Narrative Cinema." *Screen* 16:3 (March 1975): 6–18.

Nielsen, Margarete Mitscherlich. "Psychoanalytic Notes on Franz Kafka." *Literature and Psychoanalysis*. Eds. Edith Kurzwei and William Phillips. New York: Columbia University Press, 1983. 270–289.

Nietzsche, Friedrich. *Beyond Good and Evil: Prelude to a Philosophy of the Future*. Trans. R. J. Hollingdale. 1973. Harmondsworth: Penguin, 1990.

—. *The Birth of Tragedy and The Genealogy of Morals*. Trans. Francis Golffing. Garden City, New York: Doubleday Anchor Books, 1956.

—. *Thus Spoke Zarathustra*. Trans. R. J. Hollingdaly. Harmondsworth: Penguin, 1990.

Norris, Christopher. *Deconstruction: Theory and Practice*. London and New York: Routledge, 1993.

—. "Lost in the Funhouse: Baudrillard and the Politics of Postmodernism." *What's Wrong with Postmodernism: Critical Theory and the Ends of Philosophy*. New York: Harvester Wheatsheaf, 1990. 164–193.

Olivier, Christiane. *Jocasta's Children. The Imprint of the Mother*. Trans. George Craig. London and New York: Routledge, 1989.

Otto, Rudolph. *The Idea of the Holy: An Inquiry into the Non-rational Factor in the Idea of the Divine and its Relation to the Rational*. 1923. Trans. John W. Harvey. London, Oxford, and New York: Oxford University Press, 1958.

Ovid. *Metamorphoses*. Ed. G. P. Goold. Trans. Frank Justus Miller. Cambridge, Massachusetts: Harvard University Press, 1977.

Plath, Sylvia. *Ariel*. New York: Harper Colophon Books, 1961.

Politi, Jina. "The Skilful Lie" and "The Novel and Its Presuppositions." *The Novel and Its Presuppositions: Changes in the Conceptual Structure of Novel in the 18th and 19th Centuries*. Amsterdam: Adolf M. Hakkert, 1976. 17–70.

Poovey, Mary. "'My Hideous Progeny': The Lady and the Monster." *The Proper Lady and the Woman Writer: Ideology as Style in the Works of Mary Wollstonecraft, Mary Shelley, and Jane Austen*. Chicago and London: The University of Chicago Press, 1984. 114–142.

Quinlan, David. *Roman Catholicism*. London: The English Universities Press, 1966.

Radway, Janice. *Reading the Romance: Women, Patriarchy and Popular Literature*. London: Verso, 1987.

Ragland, Ellie. "Lacan's Concept of the Death Drive." *Essays on the Pleasures of Death: From Freud to Lacan*. New York and London: Routledge, 1995. 84–114.

Rahv, Philip. "Notes on the Decline of Naturalism." *Documents of Modern Literary Realism*. 1967. Ed. George Becker. Princeton: Princeton University Press, 1973. 579–590.

Rank, Otto. *The Double. A Psychoanalytic Study*. Ed. and Trans. Harry Tucker. New York: New American Library, 1979.

Rice, Philip, and Patricia Waugh. *Modern Literary Theory: A Reader*. 1989. London: Edward Arnold, 1993.

Riviere, Joan. "Womanliness as a Masquerade." 1929. *Formations of Fantasy*. Eds. Victor Burgin et al. London: Routledge, 1986. 35–44.

Robins, Bruce. "Death and Vocation: Narrativizing Narrative Theory." *PMLA* 107 (January 1992): 38–50.

Rose, Jacqueline. *Sexuality in the Field of Vision*. London: Verso, 1986.

Ross, Andrew. "Baudrillard's Bad Attitude." *Seduction and Theory: Readings of Gender, Representation, and Rhetoric*. Ed. Dianne Hunter. Urbana and Chicago: University of Illinois Press, 1989. 214–225.

Ruether, Rosemary Radford. "Strange Bedfellows: Women and Other Aliens." *New Woman New Earth: Sexist Ideologies and Human Liberation*. Minneapolis: The Seabury Press, 1975. 87–130.

Saint Augustine. *On Christian Doctrine*. Trans. D. Robertson, Jr. Indianapolis: The Bobbs-Merrill Company, 1976.

—. *On Free Choice of the Will*. Trans. A. Benjamin, and L. Hackstaff. Indianapolis: The Bobbs-Merrill Company, 1964.

Sanday, Peggy Reeves. "Conquerors of the Land Flowing with Milk and Honey." *Female Power and Male Dominance. On the Origins of Sexual Inequality*. 1981. Cambridge: Cambridge University Press, 1988. 215–231.

Scarry, Elaine. *The Body in Pain. The Making and the Unmaking of the World*. Oxford: Oxford University Press, 1987.

Schafer, Roy. "Narration in the Psychoanalytic Dialogue." *Critical Inquiry* 7.1 (autumn 1980): 29–53.

Scholes, Robert. "Who Cares About the Text?" *Literature in the Modern World: Critical Essays and Documents*. Ed. Dennis Walden. Oxford: Oxford University Press, 1990. 63–67.

Schor, Naomi. *Reading in Detail. Aesthetics and the Feminine*. New York and London: Methuen, 1987.

Sedgwick, Eve Kosofsky. *Epistemology of the Closet*. Hertfordshire: Harvester Wheatsheaf, 1991.

Shakespeare, William. *The Comedy of Errors*. Ed. R. A. Foakes. London and New York: Routledge, 1994.

Shelley, Mary. *Frankenstein; or, The Modern Prometheus. Three Gothic Novels*. 1968. Ed. Peter Fairclough. Harmondsworth: Penguin, 1986. 257–497.

Showalter, Elaine. *A Literature of Their Own: British Women Novelists from Brontë to Lessing*. London: Virago Press, 1978.

—. *The Female Malady: Women, Madness and English Culture, 1830–1980*. London: Virago Press, 1985.

Silverman, Kaja. "The Subject." *The Subject of Semiotics*. New York: Oxford University Press, 1983. 149–193.

Sjöö, Monica, and Barbara Mor. "Women's Culture and Religion in Neolithic Times." *The Great Cosmic Mother: Rediscovering the Religion of the Earth*. San Francisco: Harper and Row, 1987. 87–228.

Smart, Ninian. "Italian Catholicism and its Cousins." *The Phenomenon of Christianity*. London: Collins, 1979. 31–47.

Sölle, Dorothee. *Thinking about God: An Introduction to Theology*. Philadelphia: Trinity Press International, 1990.

Starhawk. *The Spiral Dance: A Rebirth of the Ancient Religion of the Great Goddess.* San Francisco: Harper and Row, 1979.

—. "Witchcraft and Women's Culture." *Womanspirit Rising: A Feminist Reader in Religion.* Eds. Carol Christ and Judith Plaskow. San Francisco: Harper and Row, 1979. 259–268.

Steiner, Wendy. "When you Die you'll Go to Hell." *London Review of Books* (May 1993): 19–20.

Suleiman, Susan. "Naming and Difference: Reflections on 'Modernism versus Postmodernism' in Literature" and "The Presence of Postmodernism in British Fiction: Aspects of Style and Selfhood." *Approaching Postmodernism: Papers Presented at a Workshop on Postmodernism, 21–23 September 1984, University of Utrecht.* Eds. Douwe Fokkema and Hans Bertens. Amsterdam and Philadelphia: John Benjamin's Publishing Company, 1986. 255–270.

Taylor, Mark. *Erring: A Postmodern A/Theology.* Chicago and London: The University of Chicago Press, 1987.

Thornton, Laurence. "Narcissistic Consciousness." *Unbodied Hope: Narcissism and the Modern Novel.* London and Toronto: Associated University Presses, 1984. 21–42.

Todd, Richard. "The Presence of Postmodernism in British Fiction: Aspects of Style and Selfhood." *Approaching Postmodernism: Papers Presented at a Workshop on Postmodernism, 21–23 September 1984, University of Utrecht.* Eds. Douwe Fokkema and Hans Bertens. Amsterdam and Philadelphia: John Benjamin's Publishing Company, 1986. 99–117.

Trask, Haunani-Kay. "Introduction." *Eros and Power: The Promise of Feminist Theory.* Philadelphia: University of Philadelphia Press, 1975.

Turner, Jenny. "She Who Can Do No Wrong." *London Review of Books* 6 August 1992: 8–10.

Ulanov, Ann Belford. *The Feminine in Jungian Psychology and in Christian Theology.* Evanston: Norhtwestern University Press, 1971.

Van Buren, Jane Silverman. *The Modernist Madonna. Semiotics of the Maternal Metaphor.* Bloomington: Indiana University Press, 1989.

Vellacott, Philip. *Ironic Drama. A Study of Euripides' Method and Meaning.* Cambridge: Cambridge University Press, 1975.

Vernant, Jean-Paul. *Mortals and Immortals. Collected Essays.* Ed. Froma I. Zeitlin. Princeton, New Jersey: Princeton University Press, 1992.

Vickery, John. *The Literary Impact of* The Golden Bough. Princeton, New Jersey: Princeton University Press, 1973.

Walder, Dennis, ed. *Literature in the Modern World: Critical Essays and Documents.* Oxford: Oxford University Press, 1990.

Walker, Barbara. *The Woman's Encyclopedia of Myths and Secrets.* San Francisco: Harper, 1983.

Waugh, Patricia. *Feminine Fictions: Revising the Postmodern.* London and New York: Routledge, 1989.

—. *Metafiction: The Theory and Practice of Self-conscious Fiction.* New York and London: Methuen, 1984.

Webster, John. *The Duchess of Malfi. The Norton Anthology of English Literature.* Vol. 1. 5th Ed. Eds. M. H. Abrams et al. New York and London: W. W. Norton and Company, 1986. 1240–1319.

Weedon, Cris. *Feminist Practice and Poststructuralist Theory.* New York: Basil Blackwell, 1987.

Wilkins, John. "The State and the Individual: Euripides' Plays of Voluntary Self-sacrifice." *Euripides, Women and Sexuality.* Ed. Anton Powel. London and New York: Routledge, 1990. 177–194.

Williams, Raymond. *Marxism and Literature.* Oxford: Oxford University Press, 1977.

Winterson, Jeanette. *Oranges Are Not the Only Fruit.* 1985. London: Vintage Books, 1991.

—. *The Passion.* 1987. Harmondsworth: Penguin, 1988.

Woolf, Virginia. *A Room of One's Own.* Harmondsworth: Penguin, 1975.

Worton, Michael, and Judith Still, eds. "Introduction." *Intertextuality: Theories and Practices.* Manchester and New York: Manchester University Press, 1990. 1–44.

Wynn, M. Thomas. "Cotton Mather's *Wonders of the Invisible World*: Some Metamorphoses of Salem Witchcraft." Ed. Anglo Sydney. *The Damned Art: Essays in the Literature of Witchcraft.* London, Henley, and Boston: Routledge and Kegan Paul, 1977. 202–226.

Young, Robert. "Post-Structuralism: An Introduction." *Untying the Text: A Post-Structuralist Reader.* Ed. Robert Young. Boston, London, and Henley: Routledge and Kegan Paul. 1981. 1–28.

Zweig, Paul. *The Heresy of Self-love: A Study of Subversive Individualism.* 1968. Princeton, New Jersey: Princeton University Press, 1980.

Index

About the Author

FOTINI E. APOSTOLOU is Lecturer in English Literature at the Aristotle University of Thessaloniki. Her interests are in the 18th- and 19th-century British novel. She has published on postmodern and feminist trends in the works of contemporary British novelists.